360–DEGREE
FEEDBACK

Peter Ward is a graduate in modern languages from Durham University. After taking his degree he held a number of human resource positions in the motor industry, including management training manager at Chrysler UK, international training manager at Leyland/Jaguar, and engineering personnel manager at Austin Rover. In 1985 he began work as group training director with Tesco, into which he introduced 360-degree feedback for the training of store managers. He is now a partner at Ward Dutton Partnership, which specialises in human resource assessment and development and in quality management. Since setting up the firm with John Dutton in 1991 Peter has led the development work on 360-degree feedback. Among his other assignments, he is the technical director of the Coca-Cola Retailing Research Group and provides consultancy services for several major organisations in industry, commerce and public services.

developing practice

The Institute of Personnel and Development is the leading publisher of books and reports for personnel and training professionals and students and for all those concerned with the effective management and development of people at work. For full details of all our titles please telephone the Publishing Department on 0181 263 3387.

360-DEGREE
FEEDBACK

Peter Ward

INSTITUTE OF PERSONNEL AND DEVELOPMENT

To Barney

Design by Paperweight
Typeset by Action Typesetting, Gloucester
Printed in Great Britain by
The Cromwell Press, Wiltshire

British Library Cataloguing in Publication Data

A catalogue record for this book is available from the British Library

ISBN 0-85292-705-3

INSTITUTE OF PERSONNEL
AND DEVELOPMENT

IPD House, Camp Road, London SW19 4UX
Tel: 0181 971 9000   Fax: 0181 263 3333
Registered office as above. Registered Charity No. 1038333
A company limited by guarantee. Registered in England No. 2931892

CONTENTS

ACKNOWLEDGEMENTS

I would like to express my appreciation to the many colleagues who have contributed advice or material for this book. In particular my sincere thanks to Lorenza Clifford for her contribution to the sections on validation and best practice and for her editing skills, to my Partner John Dutton for his support and insights throughout the project, to Alan Combes for his inputs on Total Quality Management, and Daniel Brown, hunter of quotations. A very special thank you goes to Bridget Cleal for her untiring work at the keyboard over several months.

My thanks also go to those who contributed and approved the case studies in Part IV: Peter Stemp and Harvey Bennett of the Automobile Association, Stephen Cole of Total Oil Marine, Walter Goodlett and Patsy Wolf of PRC/Litton, and Eva Palmer of London Borough of Croydon. Further case studies were contributed or approved by Howell Schroeder of Ashridge Management College, Ray Barker of Avon Rubber, Barrie Brown, consultant to BAA, Gordon Addision of Bank of Scotland, Andrea Kunz of Baxter Healthcare, Richard Killick of Coopers & Lybrand, Adrian Hughes of Lloyds TSB, Barbara Fothergill Independent Occupational Psychologist and Jackie Evans of the National Grid Company, and Bill Cook of Stakis Casinos.

I am grateful to the three colleagues who contributed to Chapter 9, The Future, and who have given permission for other material and illustrations to be reproduced: Thresa McDade and her team from Feedback Plus, Larry Cipolla of CCI Assessment and Development Group and Mike Perrault of Advanced Teamware Publishing. Mike also supplied the ARCO case study.

INTRODUCTION

Extracts from three conversations

Circa 1980

Boss 'Well Bernard, I think you've had a pretty good year. Your department's sales have met targets, although I was expecting a little extra. I was impressed by the performance on the Smithson's contract, although there have been one or two delays on a couple of your projects. You have controlled costs very well and have met your budgets. What do you think?'

Bernard 'Yes, I think I've done well too. There are reasons for the project delays. Whatever I do, I can't get total co-operation from everyone in other departments, and that is what's causing the problem.'

Boss 'Well, you certainly seem to get on with me all right. Generally speaking things look OK to me. Now let's have a look at my targets for you to meet next year.'

Circa 1990

Boss 'Carol, I'd like to hear your views on how you and your team have performed this last year. Tell me the highs and lows for you, how you think you yourself have improved, and any areas for further development.'

Carol 'This has been a pretty good year for me and my team. We were able to deal with everything you threw at us, and that was quite considerable. The Danish assignment was completed on time and to a high degree of quality. Our client himself commented on this, and I think we can expect some repeat business. The team as a whole were very motivated by this, and this helped to keep us going in the more difficult periods. We have managed to keep costs to a minimum this year, although next year might prove less manageable – at least in that respect.'

Boss 'I agree. You seem to be very good at managing your team and managing the client.'

Carol 'Thank you. The competency exercise we did last year really brought home to me the areas of my job and my own performance that I need to concentrate on.'

Circa 2000

Boss 'Well, Mary, it's time to review your performance again. It doesn't seem like six months since last time, but I'm sure there's lots to talk about. Putting 360-degree feedback on to the firm's Intranet has made the exercise quicker to do, and given us lots of information to discuss. But first, how do you feel about the results you and your team have achieved recently?

'Now, if you'd like to bring up your 360-degree info on the screen you can take me through what you consider to be the key points.'

Mary 'Here we go then. When I look at task-related competencies like planning, prioritising and critical thinking I'm surprised by the difference between how I rate myself and how my staff rate me. Their scores are quite a bit lower than mine. I also sent the questionnaire to our key suppliers, and their scores confirm the problem. For example, the low score in this behaviour here – "Shows that he/she can see the main issues in a mass of detail" – really says it all. The charts and comments are clear, but I'm not sure what to do.'

Boss 'I remember having this problem myself some years back. One technique I used to remedy things was to write down brief notes during the conversation, and to summarise them immediately afterwards to my colleagues. This helped me to concentrate on the big picture as well as the detail, and gave me some immediate feedback on how well I had done it.

'What's your reaction to these scores on teamworking given by your colleagues? I never see you in day-to-day interaction with colleagues, so they are probably in the best position to judge.'

Mary 'I'd better listen because I know that from next year part of my annual bonus will be influenced by this feedback...'

If you think the last extract is far-fetched, think again. All the ingredients referred to are with us now, and will be even more evident by the year 2000. If you want to be ready for it, or ahead of the game, read on.

About this book

The aim of 360-degree feedback is to obtain performance information on an individual from those with whom they interact most – such as boss, team members and staff.

I introduced this method when I was group training director of Tesco in 1987. From a slow start it has increased in popularity as people have discovered how valuable it can be, and as the climate or culture of our industry, commerce and public services have become more conducive to using it.

There are many applications of 360-degree feedback data, and it can take many forms. Users and suppliers are proliferating. There are also real dangers in using it improperly or in the wrong situations. At the time of writing there is no nationally accepted code of practice which covers it adequately. I am therefore writing this book as a guide for the human resource practitioner, line manager, or consultant who wishes to use it to maximum effect, in the right way, and in the right situations. I have been as explicit as possible about what experience has taught my colleagues and myself to be effective ways of selecting, designing, communicating and implementing 360-degree feedback.

The book is in four parts, reflecting the four aspects that we regard as most important.

Part I is an introduction for those who are unfamiliar with the technique. It deals with the most commonly asked questions, such as:

☐ What is it?
☐ Who participates in it?
☐ What can it be used for?
☐ What impact can it have on the organisation?

☐ What is in it for the individual?

☐ What is the 360-degree feedback process and how long does it take?

☐ What forces have combined to bring it to prominence lately?

Part II is very much the practitioner's guide. It covers the practical detail of how to:

☐ design questionnaires

☐ validate a 360-degree feedback process

☐ choose report formats

☐ organise data collection

☐ carry out facilitation

☐ encourage action-planning

☐ plan and implement a project.

Part III is a short, but important, section that discusses what the future holds for this technique. Although 360-degree feedback has been in existence in the USA since the late 1970s and in the UK since the early 1980s it has only come to the fore here in very recent years. What does the future hold in terms of applications of the technique, implications for the organisation and the human resources function, and technology?

These first three parts to the book contain several examples of what forward-thinking organisations are doing. However, Part IV contains five major case studies on large-scale applications: organisation development and culture change, team-building, performance development and career development, remuneration, and evaluation of development activities.

The aim, therefore, is to provide information and advice for anyone who has an interest in the 360-degree feedback field, be they a top-level human resource policy-maker or strategist, a designer, a facilitator, a project manager, or someone who just wants to get started.

The team with whom I work has experience of 360-degree feedback going back 20 years. Our journey over that time has provoked a mixture of feelings: excitement, tension, interest, frustration, satisfaction, curiosity – but above all, enjoyment. Enjoy your journey.

PART 1

ABOUT 360-DEGREE FEEDBACK

1

WHAT IS 360-DEGREE FEEDBACK?

[Horses] have always understood a great deal more than they let on. It is difficult to be sat on every day by some creature without forming an opinion of them. On the other hand, it is perfectly possible to sit all day, every day, on top of another creature and not have the slightest thought about them whatsoever.

Douglas Adams, *Dirk Gently's Holistic Detective Agency*

What's in a name?

360-degree feedback defined

Many labels have been applied to 360-degree feedback. Here are some of the most common:

☐ multi-rater feedback
☐ all-round feedback
☐ 360-degree feedback
☐ 360-degree appraisal
☐ 540-degree feedback
☐ 400-degree feedback
☐ 180-degree feedback
☐ peer appraisal
☐ upwards feedback.

All these terms represent different ways of describing the same thing. The numbers indicate the different rater groups used. Thus 180-degree feedback describes top-down and bottom-up feedback, whereas numbers greater than this imply feedback

Key points

- □ 360-degree feedback is defined as 'The systematic collection and feedback of performance data on an individual or group derived from a number of the stakeholders in their performance'.
- □ The technique measures in detail the behaviours and competencies shown by the individual or group in achieving goals.
- □ Participants can be confidentially assessed by themselves, their boss, their staff, team members, internal/external customers, suppliers, family and friends.
- □ Raters or 'respondents' judge what they perceive as behaviour, not the intentions behind it.
- □ The feedback data has many uses, including development, appraisal, teambuilding, validation of training, organisation development, and remuneration.
- □ The technique presents feedback in a powerful way, and can impact on the quantity and quality of performance data, communications, staff motivation, and the roles of those involved.
- □ Everyone's results are a mixture of strengths and areas for development, some expected and some unexpected.
- □ 360-degree feedback is not a quick process. There are important stages after feedback has been collected and reported on which are essential for changing behaviour.
- □ 360-degree feedback has become popular recently because of changes in what organisations expect of their employees, increasing emphasis on performance measurement, changing management concepts and more receptive attitudes.

from more groups across the organisation. In 1993 I coined this definition which applies to all the terms:

> The systematic collection and feedback of performance data on an individual or group, derived from a number of the stakeholders in their performance.

To explain: the data collection is *systematic*, ie done in some systematic way via questionnaires or interviews. This formalises people's judgements coming from the natural inter-actions they have with each other. There is both a *collection* and a *feedback* process; data is gathered and then fed back to the individual participant in a clear way designed to promote understanding, acceptance, and ultimately changed behaviour. The performance of either an *individual* or a *group* can be measured. The process has only recently been applied to groups or teams but can be an effective way of measuring inter-actions within the team, or team outputs and quality as perceived by customers. The sources of data are the *stakehold-ers* in the participant's (the person being rated) performance. Stakeholders are people (we call them 'respondents') who are both affected by your performance and deal with you closely enough to be able to answer specific questions about the way you interact with them. In addition to the traditional players in assessing performance we now include people such as your reporting staff, your fellow team members, members of a committee you might sit on, and your internal customers.

Two words which you might have expected to see in this defi-nition are 'confidential' before 'systematic', and 'anonymously' after 'derived'. I have omitted them deliberately because noth-ing can be totally confidential in a business organisation. It can also be argued that some organisations could cope with

Figure 1

STAKEHOLDERS

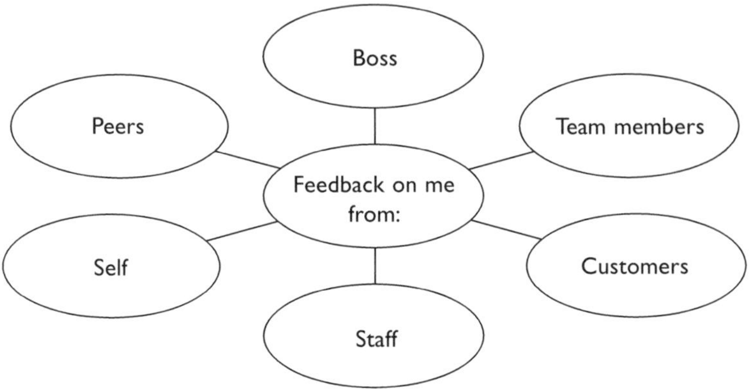

completely free performance feedback where the respondents are happy to be identified with what they have said. These are big issues to which I shall return in later chapters.

A final observation: the word 'performance' appears twice in the definition. However, we should be quite clear on the fact that it refers to the quality of a person's interactive processes or their behaviour, rather than the results they produce. This is deliberate and again is explained later.

Now go back and look again at the three conversations recorded in the introductory chapter. Let us see what elements of 360-degree feedback are involved.

The extract from 1980 has no real 360-degree elements. It is almost entirely results-oriented. There is basically only one stakeholder (the boss) who is handing out judgements. This is a situation which has happened many millions of times and is typical of the way that people give and receive feedback.

In the 1990 extract things have changed a little. There are now three respondents giving feedback. The boss has given the employee more opportunity to state how she herself sees her performance. There is also a reference to what the customer thinks. The conversation is still primarily about results (time, costs etc) but notice Carol's reference to competencies. An element of process is entering here. Notice also how the boss comments on Carol's management of her team, but how does the boss know about this?

So, we have moved on but not, it seems, very far.

Now go to 2000. The discussion here certainly touches on results (as seen by boss and employee) but there are several other respondents in the picture (the staff and the peers) giving information on Mary's style of dealing with them or how they perceive her behaviour. The feedback information is very specific and behavioural. Notice that the boss does not seem to be handing down judgements here but acting more as a coach and adviser to provide help with a performance issue.

We have therefore moved from top-down, single stakeholder, results-only measurement to something much more multi-dimensional and process-oriented. This is a true 360-degree situation.

Now let me try to answer some of the questions people first ask about 360-degree feedback.

What does it actually measure?

Many organisations have developed sophisticated ways of measuring their success as corporate entities, the achievements of departments and teams and the contribution of individuals. Most companies are able to measure their success in terms of production, sales, profits, market share, return on capital employed, or achievement of business plans. Departments, whether line or staff, tend to be measured by the attainment of strategic or short-term objectives such as annual targets, control or reduction of costs including headcount, and implementing procedures for improving efficiency. Individuals have traditionally been assessed on a micro-version of this, ie achievement of annual targets or other results.

None of these issues is normally measured by 360-degree feedback. Why do so when better ways already exist?

Other types of measurement are emerging, for example:

☐ the tendency when assessing individuals to look not just at the results achieved – but *how* they were achieved

☐ the increasing emphasis by organisations on measuring employee opinions on a number of issues, such as communications or morale, achievement of corporate standards of behaviour or values

☐ the use of external measures by organisations to assess how others see them from outside, typically using market research or other forms of survey to assess customer satisfaction. Some are asking for similar feedback from their suppliers

☐ the assessment of teams and departments by looking at what happens within the group-communication and decision-making processes. This data is coupled with the views of internal customers and others on team quality and service

☐ the increasing use of business excellence models as part of the total quality movement and the need to have more precise, data-focused ways of measuring them.

Any or all of these circumstances may be suitable candidates for 360-degree feedback. In practice it is used to assess how teams interact with their members and customers, and how individuals interact with the stakeholders in their performance. Thus managers can be assessed in terms of the competencies they possess, or more specifically through the detailed behaviours which constitute them.

So, in addition to results and output there is now the opportunity to measure how well managers communicate with other people. Not only that, a competency like communicating can be broken down into very specific behaviours, such as listening, writing, giving presentations and influencing.

Treating behaviour at a detailed level enables the respondent to think about the participant's actions in very precise terms. It helps the participant to focus on the exact areas where they need to change.

So far, 360-degree feedback has concentrated on people who are at more senior levels in the organisation, for example: directors, managers and senior executives in companies, partners or principals in the professions. However, as organisations are beginning to appreciate the power and value of such measurement, other jobholders are now finding that their behaviours are coming under the microscope: engineers, pilots, sales people, human resource professionals, customer service staff, secretaries and supervisors have all participated in this assessment and feedback process.

Who does the assessment?

The answer to this is 'anyone who works with the participant closely enough to form a view'. The list of potential respondents is long and is growing as more potential assessors emerge.

Yourself: a key feature of 360-degree feedback is that participants have the opportunity to measure how they perceive themselves and then compare this with the perceptions of others. Thus the 'Self' invariably becomes one of the respondents.

Boss: the boss has traditionally been a source of performance feedback both formally and informally. 360-degree feedback usually includes the boss. This can often contrast with the views of others.

Other bosses: if the participant has recently changed bosses then it may be that the present incumbent does not know the new one well enough to comment. In this case feedback can be sought from a previous boss. The boss's own boss can also sometimes be used, as can a functional superior.

Staff: for managers, staff provide a novel, interesting and challenging source of feedback data. This is so in traditional, autocratic structures where most communication is downward. It can be equally rewarding in more open cultures. Staff often have a different perspective on the manager's style. After all, they are on the receiving end of it, and that is a good qualification to give feedback on it. Contrast this with the views of the boss. How often does the boss actually see a manager interacting with people? They can be told about it by the manager or by others, but that is not a substitute for witnessing it. The boss is often left only with the manager's own account of how he or she manages people. Yet this can be coloured by intentions and rationalisations rather than a precise, behavioural self-description. The process of 360-degree feedback can expose managers who are good at managing upwards but not so good at managing downwards.

   While direct reports are the usual source of staff feedback data, some managers also encourage second-level reports to comment, provided these are close enough to have an informed view.

Team members: in a team culture where people interact with each other continually the observations of team colleagues can be invaluable. Indeed, some 360-degree assessments concentrate exclusively on how the participant demonstrates team skills.

Peers: this refers to those who are on approximately the same level as the participant but who may come from different departments or areas of the organisation. It can include people who go to the same meetings, and provide advice or other services. In a matrix organisation, or one in which project work is common, the choice of respondents can widen to include both permanent and temporary team colleagues.

Internal customers: these are people within the organisation to whom the participant provides a service. The spread of total quality management principles has dramatically changed the way that parts of the organisation view those whose role it is to provide them with a service. Such people provide a revealing source of feedback data.

External customers: rather than the traditional customer satisfaction survey, these people are asked specific behavioural questions about the company contacts with whom they deal.

Suppliers: internal or external suppliers gain insights which can be surprising. Much research has been conducted into decision-making styles. Some recent work by Driver, Brousseau and Hunsaker (1993) has found that people operate in two modes. A person's 'role style' is the way in which they think and interact when they are conscious of what they are doing, when they know that others are observing them, or when they see themselves as being in a formal situation. A person's 'operating style' describes how they act when these constraints are apparently absent and they feel that they can 'be themselves'. No criticism of either style is intended here; it is just a fact of life. Suppliers often find themselves on the receiving end of their customers' operating styles, of which their customers are not conscious. Feedback based on these observations can therefore be very powerful.

Friends and family members: very often those people who are closest to us socially can provide valuable insights into relevant work behaviour. On many occasions I have heard a participant say 'When I showed this to my wife she said, "I could have told them that myself"'. This group of respondents is particularly useful when it comes to commenting on issues to do with career preferences and the potential to carry out other types of work. They are also very good at observing operating styles, because their observations usually take place in a situation where the participant feels there are fewer constraints on them.

Another source of feedback is often a collection of people taken from a mixture of the groups described above. As such it is a less useful source of feedback. This is not because the respondents are lacking in knowledge or observation. It is rather that the diversity of interests and contacts of those who are being asked is obscured. One of the key features of 360-degree feedback is that different groups can often hold contrasting views of us. The boss and staff can have different opinions, or two different groups of staff can see a person differently. With some groups the relationship might be satisfactory, but other people might want us to change considerably. If this heterogeneous group is used then it becomes difficult to know precisely to whom our changed behaviour should be directed.

Can people's perceptions be trusted?

Many organisational thinkers believe that perception is reality. In other words what your colleagues see you doing or hear you saying is real to them, describes the person you are, and forms the basis of their opinion about you. It also governs how they respond to you. No matter what your own intentions are, people usually see only the tip of the iceberg. See the example in Table 1.

The answer is 'It *is* the same person' but to the staff he was two different but equally real people. The perception of both sets of staff was undoubtedly accurate. To them John's behaviour as a manager was real, but would have been unrecognisable by other people in a different department. People deal with what they see.

Now John might complain (and some 360-degree feedback participants do) that his intentions were different and mis-

Table I

DIFFERENT VIEWS

After a few weeks in his new department, John, the manager, was seen as abrupt, autocratic, willing to listen to others only occasionally. Staff who came to see him were dealt with impatiently and often overruled. Team meetings, which had previously been leisurely, friendly affairs became stressful as individuals were singled out for criticism. Staff were set very challenging assignments with tight timescales, and failure and mistakes were punished.

One day, a member of his previous department happened to be talking to one of John's recently acquired staff, and was amazed to discover what was happening. 'This is not the person we know,' she said. 'When he was with us the atmosphere was very relaxed, there was lots of debate about important issues, and he constantly asked our views on them. Can this be the same person?'

understood by his new staff. The view of senior management was that the new department needed a new broom to introduce new management practices and to sharpen up how individuals were performing. However, the point is that in 360-degree feedback respondents comment only on what they see, because this for them is reality. The intentions, background or reasons behind what they see might be perfectly rational and understandable – but if they remain invisible or unexplained then people will respond only to what appears on the surface.

In 360-degree feedback there are as many realities as there are respondents.

What can 360-degree feedback be used for?

A potential client said to me recently: '360-degree feedback is a solution looking for a problem.' I think he meant it as a criticism but I took it as a compliment, and this section explains why. The main reason is that it is quite simply a measurement tool which gives detailed data on performance. Data has not been available in this form until recently. The technique can indeed be applied in many areas and the details of these, together with examples and other implications, appear in Chapter 3. For now, however, I shall summarise the main uses.

Self-development and individual counselling

Many organisations are beginning to see performance improvement or personal development as the prime responsibility of the employee. In this context the role of the organisation becomes one of encouragement, and providing information and support. Organising and facilitating feedback are seen as part of this role.

Part of 'organised' training and development

The need to train people in groups has been with us for a long time, and in my view will remain. The reasons can be for convenience, eg several people who may or may not work together but who share the same training need, or for effectiveness, ie learning is best achieved in a group setting where people can interact with each other. A useful function of 360-

degree feedback is in helping participants to focus on their real training needs and attend appropriate group sessions.

Team-building

Data from 360-degree feedback can be used to help the team understand its internal processes, or how it is seen from outside, for example by customers (referred to as team-oriented team-building). It can also help individuals to see how other team members perceive them as a contributor to the group (individual-oriented team-building).

Performance management

Data from 360-degree feedback can be provided as a supplement to traditional feedback given by the boss. Attention to this during the regular appraisal cycle can reduce anxieties by making it seem less of a special event. It can also provide the appraisee with regular data to assess the extent to which performance has developed.

Strategic or organisation development

Data from 360-degree feedback can be aggregated to help human resources strategists identify sections or strata within the employee population that have specific development needs.

Validation of training and other initiatives

The main use of 360-degree feedback is currently to identify performance improvement needs. Many organisations have not yet used it to judge the success of individual, team or organisation development initiatives, but it has a major role here.

Remuneration

Some organisations have started to use 360-degree data as a means of determining part of the individual employee's pay package. This is one of the hottest topics in the area and is viewed with suspicion by some human resource departments. The pros and cons are evenly balanced.

What impact will 360-degree feedback have on the organisation?

If 360-degree feedback is planned and implemented in a thoughtful manner then the impact on the organisation will be very beneficial. However, before implementing a project it is important to consider precisely what impact you want it to have.

Quality and quantity of data

Large amounts of detailed information, not hitherto available on a person's performance, are generated by 360-degree feedback. The feedback is provided, not by full-time or part-time assessors, but by the people with whom you work on a daily basis. The location is not a room in the training centre or a hotel specially set aside for the purpose, but your everyday place of work, wherever that may be. The circumstances under which you are assessed have nothing to do with exercises or simulations. The activity is your normal work. It is not possible to get closer to real life than life itself. The nature and variety of the respondents and the face validity of the activities measured make it much easier for participants to understand what is said and use it as the basis for change and development.

Communications

The application of 360-degree feedback is an exercise in open management. Consider how the flow of communication changes. We now have communication upwards and across the organisation whereas before it may have only been downwards. What the participant does with this information can also create a more open atmosphere. I encourage some participants to share their feedback with others, particularly with their boss and their other respondents. There is evidence that those people who do this are more likely to improve their performance. Naturally, nothing must compromise the anonymity of individual respondents' answers, and some participants need a lot of coaching to help them share and clarify without seeming to threaten. However, the benefits of doing it outweigh the risks.

Motivation

Organisations introducing 360-degree feedback often find that it has a morale-boosting effect. Respondents are pleased to be asked to give their comments. This is not, after all, another employee opinion survey. The subject is much closer to home because people are being asked for their views on the behaviour and practices of someone they know well.

The feedback contains a mixture of strengths and areas for development. Obviously the former can be motivating *per se*, but for those people who try to change their behaviour and succeed there is an even greater improvement in morale.

Finally, it changes attitudes to performance, on the basis that what gets measured gets done. In other words, if an individual knows that the spotlight is switched on to a particular part of what they do, then they are more likely to throw their energies into these activities and try to perform better.

Roles

The role of everyone involved in a 360-degree project is changed – sometimes subtly, sometimes dramatically.

Participants find themselves asking for feedback information from colleagues – something they may never have done before. Furthermore, they may then share this feedback or seek to clarify it. For some people this can be a dramatic shift of style. When it is used for development purposes, the situation is a far cry from the old days of being sent on courses which may or may not satisfy particular needs. With this technique participants are in charge of their own development, and its success depends on them more than the other players.

Respondents now find themselves in a position of more influence over the participant. Instead of being a passive recipient of the participant's style they now realise that they can influence it by the feedback they give. Most respondents take this responsibility very seriously.

The boss's role can change from being the hander down of judgements on performance based on relatively limited information, to being a facilitator, coach, or counsellor. It involves not only clarifying and explaining the feedback that they themselves have given, but also working with their subordinate to draw more meaning from the feedback, to help the person accept it, and to provide suggestions for change.

For the human resources function the role implications are quite fundamental. They are also in line with other developments which are causing departments some heart-searching in terms of re-examining the way they operate, the skills and mind-sets needed, and the type of people they need to employ. The implications fall into two categories:

Strategic: 360-degree feedback provides access to performance data at a level of detail hitherto unknown. The days may be numbered of having to rely on performance appraisal ratings – and possibly assessment centre results – to take a snapshot of performance levels across an organisation or parts of it. The new information enables performance to be analysed in many different ways. Competencies and specific behaviours can be measured at different levels in different parts of the organisation. Demographic data can be collected and used to give accurate and useful perspectives on skills and performance.

The human resources function is in a much better position to measure the success of its strategic initiatives, and to use this information for better planning and implementation in the future. This, of course, works both ways. Comprehensive factual data can give evidence of failed projects as well as successful ones. As we have seen, there is now available a multi-purpose measurement tool which can be used in many of the function's activities.

Individual: 360-degree feedback also has profound implications for the skills of the individual human resources practitioner. Some people underestimate this. To act as a facilitator is to be constantly 'playing away from home'. You are helping an individual to understand, to come to terms with, and apply performance data which can arouse a variety of emotions in them because of its directness. You are in a situation where you do not know the answers and have to rely on your skills in working with the participant as a partner, drawing out their ideas, helping them make plans.

To many people this role represents a major change in operating style. You are not at an overhead projector explaining ideas or concepts or inputting knowledge. You are not behind a desk dispensing advice. You are not devising policies and ensuring they are followed. You are in a much less structured situation, one in which you may have less control than the person with whom you are dealing.

For example: my team provides a lot of training for in-company human resources specialists and consultants in the use of 360-degree assessment products, software tools, and the associated facilitation skills. The take-up rate (in terms of use of the 360-degree products after training) is sometimes not as high as we would like. Follow-up tells us that, whereas many people can easily take on board the technical and computer-related issues, they find the interpersonal skill demands of the process beyond anything they have encountered before, including facilitating other psychometric instruments.

The exception to this is where in-company personnel are used to facilitate major corporate 360-degree feedback initiatives. In these circumstances the organisation is ensuring that they operate outside their comfort zone until the new skills are firmly embedded.

The customer

The concept of identifying with the internal customer is nowadays accepted as a key role of any service provider. This is strongly reinforced by 360-degree feedback when customers or their representatives are used as respondents. Suddenly the customers have the opportunity to make their views known on such matters as reliability of service, attention to their needs, communication, problem-solving, and working in partnership as opposed to being at the end of the line. Such data is invaluable to the participant, but can also be of great strategic use to the organisation. Aggregated data can be used to determine the extent to which the organisation has espoused the concept of real customer service and whether there are still pockets of resistance.

As far as the external customer is concerned the impact is usually beneficial and very welcome. It is another opportunity to influence and improve the performance of the supplier. However, it is not always necessary or advisable to ask customers directly. Sometimes colleagues can be approached to give their perspective on customer service.

What types of information are produced?

We have already noted that 360-degree feedback describes primarily what people see us doing. These experiences fall into four categories.

The first two categories (A and B in Table 2) contain results that are expected. In other words, the participant knew or suspected that their respondents would agree with their own assessment of themselves. This in itself can be useful feedback because it reveals the extent of our self-awareness, and confirms our view of ourselves, whatever it might be. Anecdotal evidence suggests that those who have a high level of self-awareness tend to be seen as higher performers. The logic behind this is that such people can see how they 'come across' to others and adjust their behaviour in order to maximise the value of the relationship to both parties. Conversely, people without such self-knowledge may lack the information or motivation to change the way they are perceived by others.

Category A – Development areas – contains those behaviours which both the participant and other groups see as needing improvement.

Category B – Strengths – contains behaviours where everyone (including the participant) sees good performance. This feature of 360-degree feedback should never be ignored.

Our second two categories (C and D) cover feedback where the participant's score is different from those of other groups,

Table 2

EXPECTED AND UNEXPECTED RESULTS

Expected results	
A Developmental areas	B Strengths
C Discrepancies	D Hidden strengths
Unexpected results	

ie the results are unexpected. If the participant genuinely does not realise how they are coming across to different groups the feedback can therefore come as a total surprise and can take people aback. Helping people deal with this and learn from it is an important aspect of facilitation which is dealt with in Chapter 7.

Category C – Discrepancies – can represent a painful surprise to some people. Here the participant believes their behaviour to be satisfactory or effective, whereas other groups disagree.

Category D – Hidden strengths – the surprise can be very pleasant because it reveals to participants that in these behaviours they are held in higher regard by others than by themselves.

Most people's results show them to be demonstrating a mixture of weaker and stronger behaviours, either as perceived by themselves or others. It is very important when discussing feedback with people that they are encouraged to see their stronger as well as their weaker points. There may be some cultural issues to overcome here. When discussing someone's feedback with them I very often hear 'Forget about all this congratulatory stuff' – actually people often use more direct language! – 'and get to the bottom line. What are my weaknesses?' I maintain that knowing what you are good at is important as knowing your weaknesses. You can capitalise on your strengths to great effect

How quickly can a 360-degree project be carried out?

The full 360-degree feedback process is longer and more complicated than many people think. Any organisation contemplating a project should be prepared for the fact that the results are not immediate. However, they are worth the time and effort involved.

The feedback loop in Figure 2 shows the stages in the process.

Looking at the loop, we should realise that 360-degree feedback formalises a natural process of observation (Stage 1). People observe each other all the time, often unconsciously and unsystematically. They gain impressions about behaviour. Some of these are remembered while others are forgotten.

Figure 2

THE FEEDBACK LOOP

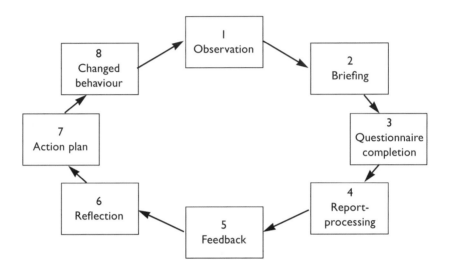

These perceptions are formed continuously in any relationship. The formalisation comes from selecting and briefing respondents (Stage 2) to think about the participant's behaviour in a conscious and structured way, usually by completing a questionnaire (Stage 3). The data is collected and then processed into a formal report (Stage 4) containing respondents' perceptions expressed in numerical, graphical or written form, which is then presented to the participant as feedback (Stage 5).

The minimum time required for these first five stages is two months, and that is after the project has been planned and communicated. Some organisations believe this is where the process ends. In fact, nothing could be further from the truth. As with any other measurement tool, the issue is what you do with the data it produces, and that part of the process does not even start until Stage 6, which I have entitled Reflection. Reflection can involve a number of actions on the part of the participant: trying to understand and accept the data by means of self-analysis, discussion with a facilitator, coaching by others including the boss, sharing feedback with others and getting clarification on points which came as a surprise or were unclear. Only when this has been done can the participant convert his or her thoughts into a meaningful and practical action plan (Stage 7) which will result in behaviour change (Stage 8). More time is then needed for the behaviour change to occur and be noticed (forward to Stage 1 again).

The whole process, from initial idea to the observation of a permanent improvement in performance, can take up to a year, and if any one stage is neglected then the results can be disappointing.

Why has 360-degree feedback become so popular recently?

The last two or three years have seen a marked increase in the interest that has been displayed in the technique. As I mentioned in the Introduction, my first exposure to the topic occurred in 1987 when I was group training director of Tesco. Slightly before that the Coca-Cola Retailing Research Council (a voluntary group of top food retailers sponsored by the Coca-Cola Company) had completed a study into the characteristics and behaviours of effective supermarket managers. This led in part to the development of a device to measure these behaviours, based on 360-degree feedback principles. I introduced this into the company for the development of store managers. At that time it was a novelty and it remained so for a number of years.

In my view, four forces have encouraged its rapid growth in recent years:

☐ changes in the role of employees and what is expected of them
☐ an emphasis on measurement within organisations
☐ the influence of new management concepts
☐ management attitudes and receptiveness.

Changes in what the organisation expects of the employee

Collaboration and teamworking are encouraged. Competitiveness is fine when directed against the outside world and opponents in the market place, but is less tolerable when directed at colleagues within the organisation. The philosophy of 'every man for himself' is no longer as strong as it was even in the 1980s. Many achievements today are the result of team efforts rather than individuals going it alone and taking all the credit. How do you assess accurately the inclination and aptitude of the employee for acting as an effective colleague or team member? You ask the people with whom the employee interacts.

The concept of continuous improvement applies just as much to the individual employee as it does to the organisation as a whole. Employees are encouraged to develop themselves and to call on the resources of the organisation to help them. The days of training departments desperately trying to fill course places for training which they thought was a good idea, but which prospective delegates or their managers clearly did not, may be over. The development needs of employees have to be much more accurately assessed so that scarce resources can be targeted more effectively.

There are other demands on the employee. Reductions in employee numbers and in levels of management, and the removal of job demarcations have meant that the remaining employees are valued for their flexibility and their ability to develop several skills. Again, traditional means of performance measurement or needs analysis are no longer adequate to determine needs and set priorities.

Emphasis on measurement within organisations

Measurement systems have proliferated in recent years. Assessing the views, suggestions, attitudes, motivations, morale, personalities, aptitudes, skills, potential and career ambitions of employees has today become a major corporate activity in its own right. Organisations want communication to be two-way; they want to listen.

Many organisations now have appraisal schemes, performance management systems, opinion surveys, briefing groups, listening groups, conferences, focus groups, benchmarking projects and development centres. In other words many, many ways of assessing, measuring and analysing employee issues are available when compared to the recent past.

Any new measurement tool that appears to be an advance on previous methods is now much more likely to be considered and used. That is what is happening to 360-degree feedback.

The influence of new management concepts

The identification and communication of what makes for successful performance in an organisation has been a prominent issue in the 1990s. The competency movement has set in motion the identification of what the ingredients of good performance are. 'A competency is a set of behaviours used to achieve a desired outcome. A competency is something you can demonstrate.' (Weightman 1994).

Many organisations have now adopted national competencies, for example those produced by the Management Charter Initiative or developed as the basis for National Vocational Qualifications. Others have developed their own. They are being used for strategic planning purposes, to improve recruitment and training, to ensure fair employment practices, and as a basis for remuneration.

The identification and description of competencies has brought about the need to measure the extent to which employees exhibit them. Previous methods of assessment are beginning to be seen as too imprecise or complicated. The detailed, behavioural, multi-dimensional approach of 360-degree feedback immediately suggests itself as an ideal measurement tool.

The study of Japanese business practices has brought about a radical re-think by European and American firms of the way organisations should be managed. One area is the contrast between results-oriented and process-oriented management. In his book *Kaizen: The key to Japan's competitive success*, Masaaki Imai (1986) describes the difference. For example, when reviewing employee performance Japanese management will take into account attitudes and behaviours. A salesperson's performance will include an evaluation of such things as time spent calling on new customers, the ratio of time spent on customer calls to clerical work, and the percentage of new enquiries converted into sales. This is process-oriented thinking because it deals with how the person arrived at their achievements, rather than just the results themselves.

Contrast this with traditional Western management thinking. In the USA, for example, rewards used to be dominated by results. No matter how hard a person worked, poor results (even if only short term) meant a low rating and lower pay than more successful colleagues. Results were everything. Yet as Western firms begin to adopt Japanese management principles, results-orientation is becoming tempered by an increasing focus on processes. This enables the reasons for performance to be analysed and improved, thus eventually improving results.

The concept of 360-degree feedback fits closely with this new philosophy because it reveals the employee's 'process', ie the behaviours they adopt to achieve results rather than the results themselves.

Management attitudes

Today's manager has adopted, or absorbed, much of the new management thinking which appeared in the 1960s. Many will not have heard of Macgregor, Herzberg, Blake, Maslow and others. Certainly when their ideas were introduced decades ago not all the ground was stony, but the concepts of open management, democracy, and adaptability had a hard time in germinating. However, they have now become part of Western management philosophy. Today's manager takes these things much more for granted.

Therefore, anything that seems to fit within their philosophy, as 360-degree feedback does, is at least tried out. Usually when it is tried out it is accepted.

References and further reading

DRIVER, M. J., BROUSSEAU, K. R. and HUNSAKER, P. L. (1993) The Dynamic Decision Maker. San Francisco, Jossey-Bass.

HUMAN SYNERGISTICS INC. (1986) Improving Store Management Effectiveness. Atlanta, The Coca-Cola Retailing Research Council.

MASAAKI, I. (1986) Kaizen: The key to Japan's competitive success. Maidenhead, McGraw-Hill.

WARD, P. (1995) Planning and Implementing a 360-degree Appraisal and Feedback Project. Unpublished paper.

WEIGHTMAN, J. (1994) Competencies in Action. London, IPD.

2

A COMPARISON BETWEEN 360-DEGREE AND OTHER MEASUREMENT TOOLS

A man cannot be too careful in the choice of his enemies.

Oscar Wilde

Key points

□ In this chapter, 360-degree feedback is compared with other measurement tools such as opinion surveys, personality inventories, performance appraisal, and development centres.

□ Criteria include: use, purpose, coverage, measurement method, administration, and respondents.

□ 360-degree feedback is unlike most other tools in that it is multi-purpose and relatively untried.

□ Like ability tests, and some aspects of development centres, it reports on behaviour.

□ Unlike other tools each participant has several respondents who can be unique to the participant.

□ As with personality inventories, there are no right or wrong answers.

□ Self-assessment is a key feature, and accuracy of self-assessment can be linked to better performance.

□ Individual feedback is required in all circumstances and has features which make it demanding to facilitate.

Using the correct measurement tool for the situation is essential. Yet there is a large array of techniques available to the human resources professional who wishes to measure aspects of the individual at work. Interestingly, the arrival of new methods does not seem to coincide with the disappearance of old ones. This further complicates the choice. I shall compare them with each other, concentrating on how 360-degree feedback fits into the picture. There are some similarities between 360-degree feedback and the other tools, but there are also some marked differences of which the practitioner must be aware.

I have used eight criteria as the basis for the comparison:

□ use – for how long the tool has been in use and how well established it is

□ purpose – the end results it aims to deliver, eg individual, team, or organisation development, selection, career planning or training

□ coverage – what the tool measures – attitudes, skills, knowledge, or perceptions

□ method – what it asks people to do, eg answer questions, demonstrate skills

□ respondents – who answers or assesses

□ mode of administration – how the assessment is organised

□ answer/score – what the answers comprise, eg ratings, right/wrong responses

□ feedback – how the participants gets their results.

The measurement tools to be compared are:

□ employee surveys
□ ability tests
□ personality inventories
□ conventional performance appraisal
□ development centres
□ 360-degree feedback.

Employee surveys

Employee surveys have become well established in the United Kingdom across all types of organisation. They enable the organisation to take its own pulse on general and specific matters. For example, they can form the diagnostic part of an organisation development or culture change project. They can cover almost anything including opinions, attitudes, communication, safety, training, leadership or morale.

The methodology is often a standard questionnaire with a combination of rated or open-ended questions. Methods can also include individual interviews and focus groups. These ask a sample of employees to give their views in a face-to-face situation, and examples of things that satisfy or annoy them.

Respondents can be anyone in the organisation. The number can be the whole organisation or a sample. Samples can also be selected from each part or stratum of the organisation. Administration of questionnaires is by mail with an explanatory letter. However, more direct means are sometimes more appropriate, eg through briefing meetings or other parts of the organisation's communication system. Questionnaires ask respondents to give their perceptions of specific issues. They rate questions on a 'how good' or 'how often' scale, or they show the extent to which they agree with a particular proposition, eg:

> Employees in this company always feel free to speak their minds.

Those who commission opinion surveys are usually the senior management of the organisation. They are the main recipients of the feedback. Other parts of the organisation, including those who have answered the questions, may not receive any feedback.

The people who are required to act on the data are usually those who commission the survey. Major surveys present so much information that there is often a considerable time lag before any action results. For example, the news that the company or its management is not trusted by the workforce is not only hard to take by well-meaning managers – it often requires several working parties and much management discussion before any decision can be taken on what to do. There is another time lag before any results become apparent. Having said that, many organisations have learnt to accept the findings and have shown determination in converting them into action.

Ability tests

Ability or aptitude tests have also become well established in medium and large organisations. Unlike opinion surveys, they are a means of aiding decisions on selection or promotion. They cover specific skill areas and provide a means for people to demonstrate the degree to which they possess a certain skill. There is only one respondent – the participant. Trained personnel administer the tests in strictly controlled conditions.

In contrast to opinion surveys, all questions have a right and wrong answer. However, feedback of results to the participant is a secondary activity. Participants do not always therefore learn how they have performed.

Examples of ability tests are verbal/numerical, reasoning, and mental or manual dexterity.

Personality inventories

Personality inventories are a prominent feature in many medium size to large organisations. Their use is in decision-making for selection and also in development and counselling in areas such as leadership training and personal awareness. They cover personality or cognitive style by inviting participants to state their preferences or what they would do in particular situations.

Personality inventories are sometimes self-administered, and sometimes administered in controlled conditions. There are no right or wrong answers and feedback is generally given face-to-face by a trained facilitator. Examples of personality inventories are 16 PF and Myers-Briggs® Type Indicator.

Performance appraisal

Most organisations have some form of performance appraisal, although it can vary greatly in terms of sophistication. The organisation uses it to help in the management and development of the individual. In his book *Appraisal* Clive Fletcher (1993) describes several applications. These include:

☐ making reward decisions
☐ improving performance

- motivating staff
- succession planning
- identifying potential
- promoting a manager–subordinate dialogue
- formal assessment of unsatisfactory performance.

Traditional performance appraisal has received criticism over the years as inaccurate, subjective, and a chore. Yet it remains by far the most widely used method of assessing performance. It is in widespread use in most organisations in one form or another.

Performance appraisal can be results-based or competency-based. It can also be a combination of both. Appraisal of results probably has its roots in the Management by Objectives movement of the 1950s and 1960s. It involves a discussion between manager and subordinate on what the latter has achieved over a given period, and will be achieving in the future. Other objectives can include performance improvements in specific areas. By contrast, the competency-based approach involves rating behavioural attributes thought to be essential to good performance. Examples are strategy, drive, relationships and persuasion.

The methodology usually comprises individual preparation by boss and appraisee, including the completion of an appraisal or self-appraisal document. The appraisal discussion then follows.

Development centres

Development centres have achieved prominence in the last 15 years or so. In an article in *People Management* Griffiths and Goodge (1994) identified three generations of development centres. First generation development centres (known originally as assessment centres) assessed the suitability of candidates for a job. In other words they were, and are, primarily a selection device. Later versions have paid more attention to potential and the needs of the participant, including feedback, counselling, and assistance with development plans.

Development centres use competencies that the organisation sees as critical to a particular job or level of job. The methods used to assess them consist of a range of techniques:

interviews, ability and personality assessment, performance appraisal information, simulations and exercises. This array of measurement tools aims to provide several ways of assessing particular competencies and therefore show more than one aspect of each one.

Respondents are a specially selected and trained group of assessors drawn from the human resources department, line management, and external expert sources such as psychologists. They base their judgements on all the various assessment methods being employed. In some versions participants also assess each other, for example by ranking each other in group discussion exercises.

Development centres can last for several days and may be complex to administer. There is usually a chairperson or organiser. In the later versions feedback is given to participants after each exercise and the organisers pay considerable attention to planning and monitoring development afterwards.

360-degree feedback

What characteristics does 360-degree feedback share with these other techniques, and in what ways is it different?

Use

Unlike the others, it is relatively new to the United Kingdom. As is often the case, the larger, more forward-looking organisations have been the first on the field, but others are catching up. In a survey in 1995 the Industrial Society found that of 237 respondents in a variety of organisations only 8 per cent claimed to be using a 360-degree feedback system. However, almost a quarter said that they were either considering it or currently incorporate some elements of it. This trend has undoubtedly continued.

Purpose

As we have already seen, 360-degree feedback has a variety of applications. It might be better, therefore, to look at those for which it is not considered suitable. The main one of these is selection. In some organisations (particularly academia or those organisations that have self-directed work teams) team members might have a say in electing those who will lead the team. However, with one or two exceptions, it is unlikely that many organisations will encourage staff to participate in the selection of their leaders. Such a concept is too foreign, however appealing it may be from an intellectual point of view.

However, it has a role to play in most other situations where the organisation wishes to measure accurately how a person is performing in their job.

Coverage
Use of 360-degree feedback covers specific areas of the job that are related to style or behaviour. This can mean more than competencies in their narrowest sense. For example, one company developed a list of values that its senior management felt it should espouse. Examples were professionalism, excellence, recognition, teamworking and safety. They commissioned a project to study how these values might show themselves in managerial behaviour. The study resulted in a 360-degree feedback instrument which senior management then arranged to be applied to themselves. This was an excellent example of the conversion of necessarily vague value statements into descriptions of 'doable' activities which people could observe. It also demonstrated a commendable desire on the part of senior management to learn whether the rest of the organisation saw them as living up to these values. Chapter 12 contains a more detailed case study on this.

Method
The method used to collect data for 360-degree feedback is almost invariably in the form of questionnaires. It shares this feature with other tests. However, data can also be collected on disk or on the organisation's computer network. I predict that as the technique becomes more widespread, then the means of collecting data will become more automated.

Respondents
This is clearly one of the main points of contrast with other assessment methods. We will therefore spend some time exploring it.

The type of respondent in 360-degree feedback differs from

those in other methods. For example, participants often have freedom to choose their own respondents, based on pre-existing guidelines. Thus the organisation might say to participants that they must approach four to six direct reports and four to six peers, but leave the choice up to them. This high degree of free-dom may not always be appropriate. A further level of control is to stipulate that they must choose reports from across all parts of the department. The next level is for the boss or the HR department to approve the choice of respondents. The ultimate level is for the organisation to specify all respondents by name, leaving participants no freedom at all. In practice, choice of respondents is usually handled more liberally than restrictively.

A frequent objection to a free choice of respondents is that it allows the participants to manufacture a result favourable to themselves. They are supposed to achieve this by approaching people who like them. There are two answers to this. The first is that 360-degree feedback encourages participants to take responsibility for their own development. This must surely include taking responsibility for the choice of whom they approach for feedback. To remove this freedom means that we are sending conflicting messages to the participant. Are they really in charge of this, or are they not? This is an example of the subtle (and maybe unwitting) ways in which organisations can prevent effective feedback from emerging.

The second answer is that it may not matter which respon-dents are chosen, providing they satisfy the main selection criterion. This criterion is simply to have worked with the participant long enough or closely enough to have developed an informed view of their behaviour. Several times, in feedback discussions with participants, I have heard people admit to having tried to secure a favourable result, only to receive an unpleasant surprise. This reaction makes sense from several angles. First, most 360-degree feedback questions are very specific, detailed behavioural statements, and the rating scales are well defined. These constraints make it less easy for someone to give a biased answer. Second, and in my view more important, having a friendly relationship with someone is not a barrier to criticising them. Someone who has my best inter-ests at heart may feel *more* compelled to give candid answers, particularly if the results cannot be traced back to them.

Conversely, someone who does not care about me, or dislikes me, is not going to take as much care over giving accurate, thoughtful answers.

In an attempt to eliminate bias, collusion, or rogue scores some processing systems use the Olympic scoring method of calculation. This method (as the name implies, it is used in judging some Olympic events) discounts the outliers, ie the highest and lowest ratings for each item. It then averages the remaining figures to calculate scores for each item. This minimises bias or potential skew to the average score from the effects of the outliers. It is also another way of protecting anonymity since there is no way to determine who from the respondent group has been eliminated. However, respondent groups have to be of a sufficient size to make the remaining information meaningful.

The final issue on respondents concerns the number of people to approach for feedback. Let us deal first with the number of respondent groups involved. In my experience the most useful number is four – self, boss and two other groups such as staff and peers.

How many should there be in each group? Unless there are exceptional circumstances I would suggest a minimum of four. Not everyone can answer all the items on a questionnaire, so when one of three respondents cannot answer, there is a danger of compromising the anonymity of the remaining two.

In theory there is no upper limit, but the practicalities of administration usually impose one. If there are more than six respondents in a group it is sometimes a good idea to sub-divide them, for example by experience, type of work, age etc.

Mode of administration
From an administrative point of view there is a danger that 360-degree feedback may get out of hand. It is certainly more complicated than other assessment methods that rely on self-assessment. If a group of 100 participants is being assessed, each one with ten respondents, then we immediately have 1,000 pieces of paper circulating in the organisation. One way to manage this situation is to make each participant responsible for ensuring that his or her respondents complete and return the questionnaire. A simple tracking sheet can be given

Table 3
360-DEGREE FEEDBACK COMPARED TO OTHER ASSESSMENT METHODS

Criterion	Employee Surveys	Ability Tests	Personality Inventories	Performance Appraisal	Development Centres	360-Degree Feedback
Use	Well established in all organisations.	Commonly used in medium size and large organisations.	Well established in medium size and large organisations.	Probably the most commonly used assessment method. Almost all organisations have some form of appraisal – however basic.	Commonly used by most medium size or large organisations.	Relatively new in Europe.
Purpose	To diagnose organisational issues, or for more specific interventions.	Selection or promotion.	Selection, development and counselling.	Performance improvement, rewards, motivation, communication, succession planning, identifying potential.	Selection, promotion and development.	Multi-purpose, excluding selection. Can be used on teams as well as individuals.
Coverage	Almost anything, eg opinions, attitudes, safety, training, quality, values.	Specific skill areas, eg verbal or numerical ability or manual dexterity.	Personality or cognitive style.	Results-based, ie achievement of objectives. Competency-based, eg demonstration of appropriate behaviours and qualities.	Behavioural competencies seen as critical to a particular job or organisational level.	Competencies broken down into detailed behaviours.
Method	Questionnaires, sometimes augmented by interviews and focus groups.	Questionnaires or exercises which invite people to demonstrate specific skills.	Questionnaires which invite people to describe their preferences, feelings, or typical modes of action.	Discussion between boss and appraisee based on appraisal documentation.	Interviews, psychometric tests, performance appraisal data, simulations, exercises.	Questionnaires on paper, disk or network.

Respondents	Answered by all or a sample of employees.	Answered by participants on themselves.	Answered by participants on themselves.	Usually boss and appraisee.	Specially selected and trained assessors drawn from line management, human resources or expert external resources.	Participant, boss and selected others, eg staff, peers, customers, team members, family members.
Administration	Questionnaires distributed by mail with explanatory letter. Answers from individuals kept confidential.	Administered by trained personnel in strictly controlled conditions.	Administered sometimes by self, sometimes in controlled conditions.	Usually organised by the HR function.	Complex administration using a variety of methods before and during the development centre.	Questionnaires usually sent out by participant. Collected externally or at a central internal point.
Answers/Scores	Questionnaires use a rating scale for perception on opinions.	Questions have a right answer. Can also have a pass or fail element.	No right or wrong answers.	Assessment by the opinion or observation of the boss and appraisee. Performance rating scales often used.	Depends on specific methods used.	Rating scales used to show perception of how effective the behaviour is, or how often it occurs. Open-ended answers also used.
Feedback	Initially to those who commissioned the survey. Sometimes to other parties.	To HR functions or line management. Not always to the participant.	Generally given to the participant face-to-face by a facilitator.	By the boss to the appraisee.	Originally to those who commissioned it. Latterly much more emphasis has been placed on developmental feedback to the participant.	Individual feedback report discussed with a trained facilitator.

to the participant, but a copy may also be held at the collection point for completed questionnaires. The collection point can then advise the participant of any stragglers and ask for them to be chased.

One of the objections some people raise about the administration of 360-degree feedback is that 'We will all disappear under a mountain of questionnaires'. In practice this does not seem to happen. It is a worry that often surfaces before a project, but which rarely arises afterwards. A more practical difficulty concerns the overloading of certain people in the organisation when it comes to completing questionnaires on others. A boss with ten subordinates who are undergoing the assessment will clearly have to complete ten questionnaires. This is unavoidable, but having short, easy-to-understand questionnaires helps a great deal. Other people, eg peers, can also be the target of too many questionnaires. One company solved this by setting a limit to the number of questionnaires that any one person was expected to complete, and asking to see the participant's nominees beforehand. It therefore managed to control the choice of respondents without appearing to be too intrusive.

Answers/scores
Unlike ability and attainment tests, 360-degree feedback does not deal with right or wrong answers – from the point of view of respondents, if not the participant themselves. In this respect it is closer to employee surveys and to aspects of development centres – notably those where the assessor observes behaviour during an exercise. As we said earlier, 360-degree feedback deals in people's perceptions.

Feedback
Some facilitators explain and hand out reports at a group session, but all facilitation should include a one-to-one session with the participant. The provision of feedback, followed by behaviour change, is the primary purpose of the technique.

Many people feel that the nature of the feedback is as demanding on the facilitator as that of a personality inventory – if not more so. There are two main reasons for this:

☐ The feedback consists of detailed behavioural statements, which, although face-valid, still need effort to prioritise, interpret and turn into development plans.

☐ The feedback comes from people whom the participant knows personally. This, however, may not stop it being quite pointed, surprising and at variance with the participant's view of him or herself. The facilitator therefore has the difficult task of helping the participant to accept and internalise the data before they can act on it.

References

FLETCHER, C. (1993) *Appraisal: Routes to improved performance*. London, IPD.

GRIFFITHS, P. *and* GOODGE, P. (1994) 'Development centres: The third generation', *People Management*. Vol 26, No 6, 40–43, June.

THE INDUSTRIAL SOCIETY (1995). *Managing best practice 17: 360° appraisal*. London, The Industrial Society.

3

THE USES AND
APPLICATIONS OF
360-DEGREE FEEDBACK

> Seeing ourselves as others see us would probably confirm our
> worst suspicions about them.
>
> Franklin P. Jones

As mentioned briefly in Chapter 1, 360-degree feedback has
many applications. More precisely, it is used for only one thing
– the measurement of someone's personal skills or processes.
The multi-use aspect stems from the fact that this measurement data, once obtained, is useful in many areas of human
resource management. In all of these the data is the same.
Although the people whose performance is measured may be
the same, the implications for the individual and the organisation are different.

Figure 3 is based on the hypothesis that some uses of 360-
degree feedback carry more risks than others. Risks, that is,
either for those administering it or for the participants in the
project. The vertical axis shows the main variable, namely
'controversy'. Another way of putting this is to describe it as
the impact of the data on the future of the individual. It is one
thing to use 360-degree feedback 'just' for development.
However, the implications of using it for pay are quite different.
The horizontal axis shows the applications of 360-degree feedback. As we progress from left to right along the horizontal axis
you will see that the degree of controversy or risk becomes
greater. This is not to say that there are *no* risks towards the
left hand side. It is just that the potential for controversy
becomes greater as you move to the right.

Key points

- □ Some uses of 360-degree feedback carry more risks than others. The implications differ with each use.
- □ Beginning a project with an understanding of the potential pitfalls helps to ensure the chances of success.
- □ With 360-degree feedback for self-development the responsibility for action lies more with the participant. The organisation should take a supportive role in the provision of solutions.
- □ Many organisations now see the technique as part of formal training programmes, this allows participants to use other course delegates as a resource.
- □ Team feedback is a relatively new development that presents a number of opportunities for improved teamworking.
- □ To make the best use of 360-degree feedback in performance appraisal, managers have to adopt different types of observation and coaching skills through proper training.
- □ Some organisations are using the technique as a driver of culture change.
- □ 360-degree feedback can be used to evaluate training initiatives.
- □ There are cases for and against using 360-degree feedback to determine pay.
- □ Total Quality Management can be supported by the use of 360-degree feedback.

I am aware that this is a somewhat negative way of looking at the process. However, if you do not know of the pitfalls in advance you are more likely to fall into them unawares. Beginning a 360-degree feedback project with your eyes open will give you a much better chance of success. So, in discussing each application I will talk about the pitfalls as well as the benefits and other aspects.

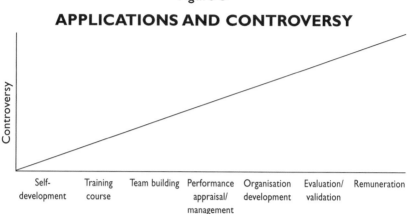

Figure 3

APPLICATIONS AND CONTROVERSY

Self-development and individual counselling

These two activities often form part of a more extensive pro-gramme, as well as being treated in isolation. Typically, an individual decides (or is recommended) to take part in a 360-degree feedback project. The impetus may be ineffective per-formance in some areas of the job, or it may be that other skills need improving if the person is to become promotable. The development needs may already have been identified in general terms, ie 'This person needs to develop in the area of people management/delegation/critical thinking', and have already been discussed with the participant. The 360-degree feedback instrument is used both as a diagnostic tool and as a stimulus for action.

The participant often receives a great deal of freedom in whom they choose as respondents, and in the type of instru-ment used. Attention is paid to tailoring not only the solution but also the diagnostic method to the individual. Thus the participant can gather data informally or formally.

The responsibility for action is very much in the hands of the participant. The organisation usually takes a supporting role in the provision of solutions, rather than a controlling or directing one. It will therefore tend to provide support, encour-agement and information. Organising and facilitating feed-back, and the provision of a choice of solutions are the order of the day.

Pitfalls

The participant may react badly to the feedback. The solution is clear briefing and skilled one-to-one facilitation.

The participant may not complete or carry out their action plan. The solution is for the facilitator to keep in contact, and for the organisation to provide continuing support.

Opportunities

Participants in self-development situations are often very keen to learn. This presents the opportunity for a close and effective relationship between participant and facilitator or with others who might be involved in the process, eg mentors or boss. The participant may therefore be willing to devote more time than usual to a deep understanding of the feedback and its implications.

Case study

The experience of the National Grid Company in using 360-degree feedback goes back to 1992 when three senior management teams took part. It was seen as extremely useful from both the individual development and team-building perspectives. In 1994 they introduced a programme around six core competencies from general manager (ie director level) downwards.

In 1995 another business within the National Grid Company took up the technique. This arose from interest within the division about using 360-degree feedback to obtain customer inputs. The primary objective was to help individuals with their own personal development planning stimulated by feedback and one-to-one facilitation conducted by an independent occupational psychologist. During the pilot stage there was a great deal of sensitivity around the process itself and some of the messages coming from it. It was the first time that some executives had received feedback from colleagues in this manner. The use of an external facilitator ensured that the feedback was accepted.

Composite data was also gathered from the individual feedback. It showed that participants had strengths in certain key competencies such as reading the business picture, commerciality, drive for achievement and self-confidence. People-orientated competencies were less strong. The quantitative data was the first hard information which confirmed the stereotype of the task-focused engineering manager. This was extremely valuable in providing a focus for training and development activities.

Other composite analyses highlighted differences between various operating groups. Again these were in line with stereotypes such as engineers working in control centres tending to have a different competency profile from those working in system development. Here again the availability of hard data made the information credible.

The approach to the feedback session ranged from 'very enthusiastic' to almost hostile. Sometimes people in the latter category eventually became the strongest advocates of 360-degree feedback. Another issue was that many participants were not used to receiving feedback that was positive and some found this hard to handle.

Frequent comments were 'I wish this had happened earlier in my career' and 'I didn't realise this was so obvious to other people. Now that I know it is, I accept I should do something about it.'

A decision was taken to separate the provision of feedback from the action planning process. This worked well; participants appreciated the time lag which allowed them to reflect on the messages and to prioritise their options for development.

Part of 'organised' training and development

Many organisations now see 360-degree feedback as part of a course or formal training programme. Participants are usually briefed beforehand and the distribution and processing take place in advance. At the beginning of the course participants receive their feedback on an individual basis. The purpose in doing this is to help participants understand their needs better and in more detail. It therefore helps the learning process by enabling them to focus more precisely on aspects of the course that are specifically relevant to their requirements.

A major benefit is that it partly solves the common problem of people arriving on the course with only the vaguest notion of why they are there in the first place.

Pitfalls

Although feedback is (or should be) given on a one-to-one basis, people might feel threatened by receiving it in a group setting. De-briefing, feedback and action planning inevitably have to compete with many other activities on a course programme. The time available for facilitation might therefore be limited. One-to-one feedback on a course is often difficult to organise without several facilitators being there, which has implications for the availability of trained resources, which may tempt some organisations to use unqualified facilitators. There may not be time for some participants to reflect on their feedback. In some cases they cannot complete their action plans because of the need to clarify feedback with respondents such as the boss.

Opportunities

Participants have the chance to use other course delegates as a resource. Formal sessions can be run in which they share their data and tap into each other's experience and skills. There is also the opportunity to share needs and development plans on an informal basis.

Case study

Ashridge Management College have been frequent users of 360-degree feedback on their courses for several years. A typical example is the Strategic Management Programme in which participants get group and individually facilitated feedback from a high-level leadership instrument. Participants find this very helpful when it comes to prioritising what they want from the course, from the tutors, and from each other. Tutors find it useful in helping participants to concentrate on their key learning points. From a strategic point of view, the college has available large amounts of composite data which gives an excellent overview of how senior managers from a cross section of the economy view their job priorities, and how their major development needs are seen.

Bank of Scotland recently introduced a management development programme for senior managers. The programme aims to encourage personal development around a number of competencies identified as essential to senior managers in order to achieve the Bank's strategic objectives.

The bank identified 360-degree feedback as an appropriate tool to gain an objective assessment of each individual's current behaviour in relation to the management competencies. The latter had been through a rigorous development process. The starting-point for this was the bank's strategic objectives. It was recognised that the feedback process would provide individual managers with a detailed analysis of their strengths, as reflected by their current behaviour. The appraisal reports would also illustrate areas where the individuals were less strong and on which they could focus their development through a personal development plan.

The participants on the senior management development programme are all currently senior managers who have been identified as having both the potential and the desire to progress to a higher level within the bank. Participants were selected from all areas of the bank and have had very different careers to date. Many participants have had wide and varied careers operating in several divisions of the bank, while others have been relatively specialised, operating within a particular role.

The participants were asked to select their own respondents within the specific guidelines of themselves, their line manager, four peers and four subordinates. Respondents were predominately bank staff, although some participants did seek responses from peers outside the organisation.

A questionnaire was developed referring specifically to the bank's competency framework. The bank had used 360-degree feedback before, albeit to a limited extent. Accordingly, those in charge of the programme were familiar with the requirement to brief the participants prior to the commencement of the process, and then to feed back the results to the participants in a controlled manner.

Participants were introduced to the process during the briefing to the programme as a whole. As the programme itself was voluntary the participants had a choice over their inclusion in the appraisal process, although inclusion within the programme meant that appraisal was compulsory. Few reservations were expressed, although in some cases people had difficulty in finding sufficient respondents who would be able to provide worthwhile feedback.

The results of the 360-degree feedback were fed back to the participants during a development workshop specifically designed for that purpose. The two-day workshop looked at several issues surrounding change within the organisation, including organisational goals and individual aspirations and motivation. Participants were then introduced to the style of the appraisal report before being given time alone to review their personal feedback. Individuals also enjoyed the opportunity of a one-to-one session with a facilitation consultant who was able to ensure that the appropriate messages were derived from the feedback and included in the development plan. Further workshops were developed based on an analysis of the feedback results.

Some organisations have taken the opportunity to run menu-driven courses which enable the tutors to respond immediately to participants' needs as identified through 360-degree feedback at the beginning of the programme. Within a given topic area for a course – say managing people – there might be nine or ten competencies such as:

☐ delegating
☐ empowerment
☐ motivating
☐ coaching
☐ mentoring
☐ team leadership
☐ managing diversity
☐ personal integrity
☐ communicating.

However, not all participants will share the same needs. Some might require more on coaching, whereas others might need more attention to team leadership. If these needs can be revealed in detail the tutors can quickly structure the programme accordingly. Thus, some sessions can be devoted to common or mandatory subjects, while others provide a choice. Clearly, this can be quite tutor-intensive, with perhaps two or three sessions happening simultaneously for individuals or small groups. It also makes demands on the flexibility and breadth of knowledge of the tutors. The result, though, is that participants do not feel that they are there to follow someone else's agenda. Instead, many are impressed that so much attention has been made to satisfy *their* requirements.

Teambuilding

Team development activities can benefit greatly from the application of 360-degree feedback. Team members can assess each other on such skills as communicating, delivering on promises, planning, listening and maintaining relationships. This is essentially an individual 360-degree approach but within the confines of the team only. In such an application the individual receives his or her feedback in advance of a team development session. In discussion with a facilitator they then decide and plan how they will react to this feedback, what they will share, and on what they will seek clarification. Sometimes standard individual instruments can be used, but there are now questionnaires that focus specifically on teamworking skills. The approach promotes individual development within teams. It uses the team not only to identify individual improvement needs, but also to help with the development itself. The ARCO case study in Chapter 11 contains a detailed example of this type of application.

Another approach, for which individual instruments are less useful, is to view the team as a unit, rather than a collection of individuals. Thus the team is treated as the 'self' with its own competencies and specific behaviours. The team can obtain feedback from a number of sources. For internal team processes such as results orientation, effectiveness of meetings, working for each other, and understanding the vision, it can obtain feedback from its own members. The team members' views can be averaged, but sometimes the team leader's views are shown separately. After receiving its feedback the team can then concentrate on those team processes that it has identified as needing attention. The feedback is so specific that the corrective actions required are quite easily identifiable.

Further feedback can come from the team's customers. Given an opportunity, those on the receiving end of a team's or department's services can provide precise and useful feedback on many aspects of their relationship. These can include how well the team communicates, the technical competency it displays, how well it delivers on promises, and its problem-solving capabilities.

Pitfalls

In the case of the individual team member feedback this can sometimes be threatening. Feedback puts pressure on team members because it may need sharing or discussing with others in a team-building session. Team unit feedback is far less threatening because it focuses on the team's strengths and weaknesses rather than those of an individual. However, the nature of all such team feedback is that it requires well developed facilitation skills in order to be acceptable to, and usable by, the team or its members. The specific and personal nature of some of the feedback puts the facilitator right at the heart of the interpersonal processes that exist within or outside the team. It requires training and experience to deal with the inevitable problems and help the team make the most of its strengths. Although the skills required to help with this feedback are almost identical to one-to-one facilitation, the process is not as easy as it may look. Some facilitators who are used to conventional teambuilding or to feedback on style descriptions derived from self-assessment, rather than behaviour drawn from 360-degree feedback, have difficulty in making the transition. The need to handle this in a team setting can be quite challenging.

Opportunities

Team 360-degree feedback is a relatively new development that presents a number of opportunities for improved team-working. First, the feedback can be gathered before any team event happens. This effectively takes the place of much of the diagnostic work that a consultant or facilitator might do beforehand. It also means that much less time is needed at the team event in trying to identify the team's strengths and weaknesses – the work is already done and the results can be discussed straight away. This leaves more time for the team to concentrate on improvement actions in specific terms, rather than coming away with a 'wish list'. It shares the other benefits of individual feedback in being much more powerful than anything team members will have seen before, and more capable of being turned into concrete actions from which the team or its members will benefit.

Case study

Lloyds TSB have used 360-degree feedback for development purposes for some time, but they have recently been experimenting with team feedback. A number of teams conducted pilots in order to gain experience of how team 360-degree feedback worked and to learn about what instruments were available, while at the same time trying to improve their own performance. Two of these were the central quality team and the OFI (opportunities for improvement) team.

Respondents were team members and internal customers, providing a combination of feedback on individual team member skills, team processes, and team outputs. One advantage of team feedback projects is that there are often communication mechanisms already in place which make briefing and other preparation easier. That was the case with these teams, who were able to set up the project using existing team meetings and other regular contacts with those outside the group. This also helped teams to maintain members' interest and awareness during the slack period after the forms had been completed but before the feedback sessions started.

Feedback was done on an individual basis using an outside facilitator, and for each team by several whole-team sessions. Below is the overall agenda which the teams set themselves for these meetings for understanding and acting on the feedback:

Introduction
- recap on the process
- objectives of this session
- feedback timetable
- roles
- ways to avoid feedback!

Feedback on team processes and outputs
- recap on questionnaires
- present team processes

- team identifies issues
- discussion
□ present customer orientation
- team identifies issues
- discussion
□ establish priorities for action or clarification

Individual feedback sessions on team member's skills

Team feedback
□ present teamview scores
□ individual sharing of feedback
- positive
- negative
- positive surprise
- negative surprise
- opportunity to clarify with the team

Conclusions
□ discuss main conclusions from each feedback type
□ draw overall conclusions
□ prioritise main areas for action
□ agree actions and review dates.

One problem encountered was in finding three- to four-hour diary slots for the whole team facilitation meetings within a reasonably close space of time. This meant that in the central quality team one or two members were absent, with a consequent effect on the value of the meeting. This problem reinforced the lesson that teams need to invest a lot of time in discussing the feedback and working on action plans as a unit. None the less, everyone participated in at least one team meeting, and the facilitator was able to bring people up to date.

The results were a greatly increased awareness of themselves as individuals and a team, and improved methods of working.

Performance management

This area of human resource management lends itself very readily to appraisal through 360-degree feedback. It is a little surprising, therefore, that this was not among the first applications. I suspect the reason is that self-development, training courses and team development are not institutional systems in the same way that performance management is. Performance appraisal, for example, usually has official documentation, requires the regular involvement of most, if not all, levels within the organisation, and has links with other systems such as rewards, assessment of potential, and career planning. Staff need training to understand the appraisal system. Managers need training to operate it. Small wonder, then, that changes to the system are not all that frequent. Nevertheless, we are now seeing increasing interest in using 360-degree feedback instead of, or as part of, conventional appraisal.

Pitfalls

The pitfalls are similar to those associated with other applications of 360-degree feedback. However, they are likely to be greater when applied to formal, regular and widespread appraisal. The main threat is that there might be a negative emphasis. We have seen elsewhere that everyone is a mixture of good and less-than-good performance, yet there seems to be a tendency for people to concentrate on the unsatisfactory issues. Despite training, many appraising managers still feel compelled to concentrate on the weaker aspects of performance, weaknesses that need remedying, problems that require solving, or faults to be ironed out. This happens despite what the textbooks tell us about balancing criticism, making it constructive, and looking forwards rather than backwards. Within the mass of 360-degree feedback data that becomes available on a person's performance there will inevitably be opportunities to punish and to find fault. Thus it might promote a culture of tale-telling, putting the boot in, and over-criticism.

The other main pitfall is that some appraising managers might have difficulty in adapting to the new demanding role which 360-degree feedback requires of the boss if it is to be carried out successfully. Let us look at how this role is different. Traditional performance appraisal is based on top-down judgement of how the employee has performed over a given period. The achievements are to do with the accomplishment of objectives. This is not to ignore the arrival of a competency approach towards appraisal, but the latter has not yet had time to become widespread. Yet to be successful 360-degree feedback asks the manager to employ a different type of observation and conceptual skill.

The manager now has to:

□ concentrate on processes as well as results
□ be more observant than they otherwise might be
□ describe the tip of the iceberg of performance
□ act as a facilitator.

This last role will present difficulties for some managers. It requires them to sit down with staff to help them understand their feedback, prioritise it, and convert it into action. Unless the organisation has an extremely large army of professional facilitators the manager will have to acquire performance management skills (identifying development needs, helping the individual to change, and monitoring performance) which many do not yet have. (Incidentally, whenever we produce group or composite pictures of performance on management competencies or skills, one in particular comes bottom of the list nine times out of ten. Yes, you've guessed – *coaching*!)

Opportunities

Fortunately the opportunities presented by 360-degree feedback outnumber the pitfalls. If handled properly in an appraisal system it can:

□ result in performance improvement
□ promote self-awareness for the participant
□ encourage self-development
□ clarify problems
□ stimulate change
□ build participants' confidence
□ reinforce useful behaviours.

Performance management systems that use 360-degree feedback *are* capable of achieving these results, provided the manager receives proper training and support to carry out a role that is much more complex than in the more conventional systems.

Case study

Stakis Casinos decided to use 360-degree feedback to enhance their performance appraisal system. This had been in place for a number of years and was used primarily for the purpose of performance improvement. They were beginning to find that development needs were becoming predictable and that appraisal information was getting very similar from one year to the next. They wanted something that would breathe new life into their system, by making the feedback come alive. They now use 360-degree feedback for branch managers, who are assessed by their area director, peers, and members of their own branch management team. The company is in the process of replacing their appraisal paperwork with the 360-degree feedback report. When processed, this goes to the participant along with a specially written summary of its contents. The boss receives a copy of the summary and uses this as an agenda for the appraisal discussion. As a result of the discussion the participant writes to the boss with a list of areas in which they intend to develop and what they plan to do.

Bill Cook, personnel manager, says:

> Our managers were becoming bored with the same old appraisal systems and target setting was predictable and uninspiring. I read about 360-degree feedback and it immediately caught my imagination. Our managers' response to 360-degree feedback has been enthusiastic and positive and targets have been focused on what drives the businesses: improve communication with staff; improve customer awareness skills; improve teamwork.

Strategic or organisation development

The reason that this application comes towards the right end of our controversy chart (see page 40) is that, whatever the effect on individuals, the organisational implications are large. Most initiatives of this type using 360-degree feedback have at their heart the behaviour change of all individuals in the organisation from the highest to the lowest. Through changing individual behaviour they aspire to change the way in which the whole organisation runs.

Pitfalls

Projects of this nature can succeed only if they have a high profile. This means starting at the top by getting senior management to give a signal about change by means of their own behaviour. For the human resources function, it means finally getting the chance to prove that changes in management style can affect the success of the organisation. Heady stuff! And if it fails, or proves to be a damp squib? Heads may roll.

The risk for the organisation itself is disillusionment resulting from failed promises of a better tomorrow.

Opportunities

Several major opportunities are open to organisations that successfully change their culture. In particular, 360-degree feedback can bring about:

- ☐ altered relationships in terms of more supportive management and better team working
- ☐ changed attitudes to performance
- ☐ changes in the ways in which people give and receive feedback
- ☐ helping to establish the concept of the internal customer.

Case studies

The Automobile Association is currently in the middle of a major project designed to change the way their managers manage. They have sampled employee opinion regularly for a number of years. One common viewpoint that emerged recently was that management practices needed revising. Updated managerial competencies were described in a document called *Management standards we can trust* which is being assessed through 360-degree feedback throughout their 700 strong management population. Further details of this major initiative appear in Chapter 10.

Baxter Healthcare is involved with culture change on a truly international level. The Company specialises in the manufacture of hospital equipment. Their products range from artificial hearts to operating masks to blood products. They decided actively to promote their corporate values – respect, responsiveness, and results – to the whole of their workforce. The

chosen instrument for this was a 360-degree feedback questionnaire in order to let individuals see how they were measuring up to these values, followed by feedback, facilitation and
support for change. The project started in the USA but is now
well under way within Europe. Baxter have factories and offices
in most European countries and there is a great deal of co-operation between nationals of different countries. However, not all
staff are able to communicate with each other in a common
language, so questionnaires have now been translated into
French, German, Italian, Dutch and Spanish. A top-down
approach is being employed, with senior people completing the
questionnaire first.

BAA plc implemented a culture-change programme in 1994
called 'Sharing the Vision'. This was aimed at senior management and emphasised the importance of leadership and self-
development in achieving the company's mission. The change
programme relies on a major training programme to achieve its
objective. A significant part of this is a rigorous 360-degree
feedback instrument. The chief executive and all the members
of the management executive underwent the 360-degree feedback instrument with feedback, as an introduction to the programme. The fact that the top team had been the first to
complete the process acted as a strong motivator and positive
indicator of the programme's value. Members of the senior
team now act as sponsors of the programme.

Evaluation/validation of training and development

Training evaluation has been a much-discussed topic over the
years. Yet, surprisingly, it is not something which organisations carry out routinely or extensively. If done well, however,
it can be of great benefit to the training and development
function. It can:

☐ give accurate pointers to how you can improve future programmes
☐ provide evidence of success to convince sceptical colleagues
☐ improve your credibility as a training professional
☐ reveal areas where participants need more attention or more
   post-training support.

In 1959 Donald Kirkpatrick developed a model which many trainers have used for evaluation purposes, if not in its entirety. He identified four areas for analysis:

Reaction

In other words, how do participants feel about aspects such as timing, programme content, administration, the effectiveness of the trainer, etc? Essentially, this is a customer satisfaction survey. It usually takes the form of a questionnaire handed out at the end of the programme for participants to complete on the spot. Cynics call this the 'happy form', arguing that it takes advantage of end-of-programme euphoria for participants to write down nice things about the training and the trainer. Many organisations use this as the only method of evaluation. Constructed properly and analysed conscientiously, however, it can yield useful information, in particular pointers for future improvement.

Learning

How much new knowledge and skill have been acquired during the course of the training? This type of evaluation takes the form of tests or simulations performed at the end of, or during, the training. Tests can be of various sorts (ranging from multiple-choice questionnaires to a full written examination). Simulations are usually observed role-plays or other exercises that require the participants to demonstrate the skills they have learned. The demonstration of skill is observed by one person, or occasionally several people.

Behaviour

This asks the questions: to what extent have participants changed their behaviour back at the workplace? To what extent has the classroom training transferred to the job itself? The main method for doing this consists of on-the-job observation and reports from the trainer, the boss or colleagues.

Results

Here we are trying to gauge the effect of changed behaviour on matters that are important to the business. These include improved efficiency, faster work rates, reduced costs, greater customer satisfaction, lower absenteeism, higher sales, or better quality of production. A variety of methods are used to measure different types of result.

Kirkpatrick (1994) points out that as you progress from reaction to results the information becomes more meaningful, but harder to gather. The latter point probably explains the results of an American Society of Training and Development survey in 1996 that showed the degree to which the four areas of analysis were used to evaluate training courses. The results were:

Reaction: 94 per cent.

Learning: 34 per cent.

Behaviour: 13 per cent.

Results: 3 per cent.

The main reason for the low focus on behaviour and results is probably that the measures are inefficient and time-consuming to carry out. In many cases they are seen as just not worth the time and expense required. However, 360-degree feedback presents a much better opportunity to improve the analysis of behaviour and results. The application to behaviour is self-evident – because that is what the technique measures anyway. It looks at on-the-job behaviour as observed by those who are close to it or who are in some way affected by it.

The 360-degree feedback format can also apply to the measurement of results. From asking respondents to comment on behaviour, it is but a small step to asking them to comment on what this changed behaviour is producing. For example, instead of asking for a rating of a person's communicating skills in the usual terms (listening, oral or written presentation, etc), we would now ask for ratings in areas such as:

☐ To what extent do you now understand what this person is saying to you?

☐ What changes have you seen recently in this person's use of vocabulary?

☐ How many misunderstandings have there been between him and others?

A critic might say that this is turning 360-degree feedback into just another staff opinion survey. Wrong; that is what it is already: a carefully designed, controlled method of asking a defined target population what they observe or think.

Here is a final thought from an ex-company trainer: many training and development activities have never been subjected to the same quality of scrutiny as some other parts of the organisation. Measurement of changed behaviour and results has been seen as difficult. Senior managers or customers have been asked to treat development activities as an act of faith, and many have done so. Strangely, the arrival of 360-degree feedback has not resulted in its use as a before-and-after measure of training and development activities. Very few organisations are using it for this purpose; I wonder why. Are acts of faith easier to live with? After all, what would happen if a cherished initiative were shown through 360-degree feedback to have had no effect at all on the behaviour of participants?

Organisations that have used 360-degree feedback to measure the effectiveness of development activities include Avon Rubber (whose programme is mentioned in the section on 360-degree feedback and total quality) and London Borough of Croydon, which is featured as a major case study in Chapter 14.

Remuneration

The most controversial application on our controversy chart is the use of 360-degree feedback for remuneration. This is perhaps less dramatic than it sounds because no one to my knowledge uses it as a 100 per cent determinant of pay. What happens is that some element of pay, let us say the annual increase, or some part of an annual bonus is determined by other people's view of performance. For example, in some parts of the financial services industry the bonus of a senior manager can be determined partly by results achieved, partly by cross-selling of other services, and partly through peer and subordinate review of their management competencies. Playing it safe? Not when you realise that the complete bonus can exceed £1,000,000!

There are many pitfalls and opportunities in this approach to remuneration. If I was having a conversation with myself about them, this is how it would go:

The proposition is: '360-degree feedback should be adopted as a major element in decisions on a person's pay or other remuneration.'

Me

Most elements of pay: increases, bonuses, etc, are in the hands of the boss, yet experience tells us that bosses are frequently not in a position to judge a person's all-round performance because they are not present when much of it takes place. How can my boss judge what sort of people-manager I am? He does not experience it; he just has my word to go on. You might argue that a boss can judge results, but so can internal and external customers.

Myself

You are over-generalising about the poor quality of management today. Some managers do have an accurate view of how their staff perform. People are there to achieve results, so what is wrong with their boss measuring them? Anyway, as one human resource manager pointed out to me recently, his organisation had a perfectly good appraisal system which had been in place for 20 years. It worked, so why change it?

Me

But we know that bosses frequently over-rate the performance of their immediate reports; they tend to rate them higher than either subordinates or even peers do. Appraisals by bosses can be biased by how well they get on with a particular individual at a personal level, especially if they are not forced to think specifically by something like a precisely-written questionnaire.

Myself

OK, but providing the boss is being consistent with everyone they are rating, then it does not matter if they are high or low raters; at least people are ranked.

Me

Ranking people into a pecking order is a very crude and possibly unfair way of determining rewards. 360-degree feedback is often felt to be more fair and accurate than other traditional methods, because it encompasses the views of all the stake-holders in a person's performance, and is regarded as more objective because it asks people specific, behaviourally-based, well researched questions.

Myself

Not so. It is all too subjective. Who says that several subjective opinions are better than one? It can all get very confusing. There is no control over who participants may choose for feed-back; they could choose only people with whom they get on or who owe them a favour. There is bound to be an element of 'you scratch my back and I'll scratch yours'.

Me

Of course it is subjective; what form of appraisal isn't? But dif-ferent views can balance each other out to give a more accurate view overall. Alternatively, the views of different respondent groups can be given more weight depending on the type of job. A service provider may be better judged by the receivers of the service; a general manager by the people they manage; a sales person by their customers; and so on.

Also, you do not have to give people a free choice over respondents. The choice can be vetted by the boss or by the human resources function. Interestingly, it seems that the make-up of a respondent group does not necessarily govern your results. Even people who like you might mention the unfavourable things under the cloak of anonymity.

Myself

Anyway, this all seems very complicated and might be far too in-tricate a system for many organisations to set up and administer.

Me

No when you look at what has to be considered in most organ-isations: different rates and hours, overtime, bonus arrange-ments, job evaluation systems, profit sharing and so on.

Myself

That argument could apply to many other reward systems. Is this really going to be a fair determinant of how much an individual gets paid? I still think that 360-degree feedback is more open to bias than other methods of appraisal.

Me

By definition, 360-degree performance measurement is aimed at what a person does rather than who they are, or what their position is. It measures the effectiveness of a person's working processes and, more specifically, how they interact with other people, not just how well they get on with the boss.

It does not have to govern the whole remuneration package. Perhaps only a certain amount of the pay award (let's say 50 per cent) might be decided this way, or perhaps a proportion of the annual bonus. The rest could be determined by more conventional means, thus giving a degree of comfort to more nervous organisations.

Myself

It sounds as though there is not as much confidence in the accuracy of the technique as people claim. Why else limit its scope? Why not apply it to the whole rewards package if you are so confident about it?

Me

Because it may not be relevant to do so and other factors need to be taken into account. The boss should clearly be the final arbiter of who gets what, and should retain responsibility. Perhaps more weight should be given to their views.

Perhaps the person is new to the job, therefore different performance standards might apply in the short term, or there may be special difficulties surrounding the job which warrant extra consideration.

Now you are the one who is over-generalising.

Myself

OK, here is a different argument: many large organisations (and quite a few small ones) are conservative and subject to tremendous inertia. This probably applies to their human resources function as well, which would face an uphill task in introducing and implementing such a revolutionary principle.

Me

Ah yes, but the new system does not have to be imposed throughout the whole organisation all at once for it to be ultimately successful; quite the opposite. The best way to handle it might be through evolution rather than revolution. It is easier to inject 360-degree feedback gradually into the corporate bloodstream by starting with less controversial applications. You can introduce it initially for development purposes, either individually or on training courses. If it becomes part of the formal performance management system, then perhaps for the first year it should be used solely for developmental needs which can be remeasured the following year. When people, participants and their respondents alike, have become used to rating each other in this way, then is the time to go forward into the link with pay, provided, of course, that we communicate these changes of use and their implications effectively. The answer, as ever, is to have systems which are obviously fair, thoroughly-documented, and well-communicated. There is, as yet, no generally accepted body of 'best practice' in this new field ... but that is another story.

Chapter 13 presents an innovative application developed by PRC/Litton of 360-degree feedback to pay and bonus.

360-degree feedback and total quality management

Here is a final application of 360-degree feedback that is quite new, and different from the others already mentioned. At the 1996 annual conference of the European Foundation for Quality Management, 360-degree feedback was mentioned four times in the first morning by major speakers. This was before an international audience of almost 1,200 people, and is symptomatic of the rapidly increasing profile of the technique as part of the total quality movement.

Current quality systems, such as ISO, Baldrige or EFQM, emphasise 'evidence' as part of their quality criteria. By focusing on competencies and gathering data on actual behaviour, 360-degree feedback can make a significant contribution in the total quality measurement area. It complements the assessment models and techniques currently in vogue by providing a depth and subtlety of analysis not available from using conventional questionnaires.

Many organisations that have embraced total quality report that the hardest part to get right is changing the attitudes and approaches of employees. The more procedural and statistical sides are easy by comparison. The 360-degree feedback approach makes the people and team issues within total quality easier to get to grips with, by acting as a catalyst for changes in performance and the adoption of a new culture.

The concept of continuous improvement for individuals, teams and organisations can be supported only by accurate measurement of where you are now compared to where you were before. The detailed, multi-dimensional perspective of 360-degree feedback is a tool ideally suited to provide this measurement on a continuing basis.

Another concept central to total quality thinking is that of the internal customer or the customer–supplier chain. The notion that, within an organisation, everyone is someone else's customer can easily be given lip service treatment, but is harder to implement effectively because of the change of mindset required. The organisation can use 360-degree feedback to structure the data collection and analysis of customer and stakeholder feedback. This allows or encourages people to receive and consider detailed feedback from their customers, rather than try to rely solely on their own – possibly too comfortable – preconceptions.

One company which has recognised the link between 360-degree feedback and total quality is Avon Rubber. They have used a total quality approach for many years, and recognised at an early stage the central importance of training and team-building in creating and sustaining quality. A particular feature of this approach involves using 360-degree feedback to help people work together more co-operatively in a team situation. Their operation in Cadillac, USA, implemented a teamworking programme based on team feedback. This involved each individual receiving feedback from their fellow team members, followed by individual and team development activities. Again, unusually, feedback was organised twice to give a before-and-after measurement, and the programme resulted in demonstrable performance improvements. A third team measurement has just been completed, but the results are not comparable because of changes in team composition. The company has carried out a similar three-stage project at its Manton plant.

In some cases the team feedback technique has been rolled out to a second level within the organisation. Managers who were team members at the first level now participated as team leaders.

The impetus gained from these projects has led the company to implement 360-degree team feedback in Mexico, Portugal and the Czech Republic. This last application, in which questionnaires had to be translated, resulted in a large breakthrough in team effectiveness following extreme suspicion initially on the part of those managers who were used to the former political and business climate.

There is a final application which may raise a few eyebrows. At one of their several UK operations the manager was due to move elsewhere. The plan was to change the job to make it more of a team-leader position in which the incumbent would bring with them their existing duties and graft on team leadership. The new team leader was to be selected from within the ranks of the existing team. Feedback from team members played a significant part in filling this position.

Reference

KIRKPATRICK, D. (1994) *Evaluation Training Programs: The four levels*. USA, Berrett-Koehler Publishers.

Part 11

DESIGNING AND
IMPLEMENTING
360-DEGREE FEEDBACK

4

QUESTIONNAIRE DESIGN

It is nonsense to say that there is not enough time to be fully informed. Time given to thought is the greatest time save of all.

Norman Cousins

Nothing is more terrible than activity without insight.

Thomas Carlyle

Key points

- ☐ This chapter begins by debating whether organisations should initially design their own questionnaires.
- ☐ Standard tests can often provide a guarantee of reliability which in-house versions cannot do.
- ☐ The value of questionnaire customisation is that one small change to a measurement tool can have a large effect on future performance.
- ☐ In designing questionnaires, the precise purpose should be identified before content domain, competencies and communication style are considered; the purpose will have a direct effect on design.
- ☐ A behavioural item shows how a participant is acting to demonstrate an aspect of the competency.
- ☐ When designing a questionnaire, specific guidelines can be followed to increase the effect of the instrument.
- ☐ Frequency, effectiveness, importance and agreement scales can be used for the measurement of rated questions.
- ☐ Open-ended questions help respondents to use their own words and give examples when describing a participant's behaviour.
- ☐ The instructions for completion and distribution of the questionnaire and the communication both to participants and respondents are important to the overall validity of the 360-degree feedback project.

Why design your own questionnaire?

Before we look at how to design 360-degree feedback question-naires, let us look at why you should bother. There are dozens of proprietary 360-degree feedback instruments on the market. Many have a good track record, and many of their distributors can produce evidence of professionalism used in test construc-tion, and thorough validation. Some are of American rather than British origin, but they measure competencies and describe detailed behaviours that are readily recognisable by British people, despite what to us are odd spellings, such as 'behavior' and 'analyze'.

The answer to the question 'Why design your own question-naire?' is 'Maybe you should not' – at least not at first. There are several reasons for this. First, the employment climate (especially in the USA) makes test constructors and users focus closely on issues of validity and reliability. The process of car-rying out statistical and other validity analysis is a necessary investment. Being able to show convincing evidence that the developer used rigorous, professional standards in devising and evaluating the questionnaire is important in itself. In a liti-gious climate the disaffected employee can and does sue the employer readily for what they consider unfair treatment. Legal scrutiny can, and no doubt will, focus on the 360-degree feed-back system, its development, and the way the user uses it. All the more reason, therefore, for using a questionnaire that you know has been through such a rigorous process. This in no way implies that British producers pay less attention to validation. Whatever the origin, standard tests can often provide a guar-antee of reliability which in-house versions cannot.

Moreover, a cynic would say that the competencies that most standard management or leadership questionnaires use are very close to those treasured sets of statements which many British companies have spent so much time and money on developing. Naturally, every company believes that there is a unique formula of factors that are critical to success in its own environment. But there has to be a limit beyond which differences between formulae amount to nit-picking. There is something to be said, therefore, for using standard question-naires which meet 80 per cent of the target, rather than paying more, in time and money, for a complete fit.

Finally, some proprietary instruments use normative scores. These enable the participant to see not just how others rate them; they can also discover how their performance compares to that of many other people.

So why produce your own?; or indeed engage someone else to do it for you? One reason is that a little judicious tailoring can make a great deal of difference. Stakis Casinos, referred to earlier, use what is effectively a standard instrument (the Leadership Assessment Survey written and published by CCI, an American publisher). However, one competency this instrument does not cover is dealing with customers. The branch manager's job is not only to manage a responsible, well-regulated operation, lead and motivate their employees etc; they deal personally with customers as their host. This latter competency is not in the Leadership Assessment Survey. We therefore added six questions on looking after customers, responding to enquiries, acting hospitably, etc. The benefits gained from the conventional management competencies in the questionnaire were basically a more detailed (and therefore more useful) description of development needs, some of which were already known. The surprises came from the results on dealing with customers. Traditional appraisal, ie from the boss, had never identified whether a manager was good or poor at dealing with customers. The boss never observed this behaviour in their normal relationship. However, staff observed it all the time. This led to development plans in important areas never dealt with before.

This example shows the value of customising. In other instances there is a strong case for starting with a completely clean sheet of paper. Coopers and Lybrand have produced a 360-degree system for use within their management consultancy division. It is part of the development of staff at principal level with a view to reaching the next and ultimate promotion – to partner. Most proprietary instruments are by their nature generic. Large numbers of sales and/or high prices are required to justify the investment in development and validation. Something too specialised is hardly likely to produce huge sales. The unique combination of competencies required of a partner in a major management consultancy firm is not close to anything a generic instrument could measure. Therefore a tailor-made version is essential.

There are other factors that influence the choice. As we said in Chapter 1, 360-degree feedback measures process, not results. There are a large number of questionnaires that measure various aspects of management processes and those of other employees, particularly where they deal with interactive skills such as communication, influence, etc. The choice will depend on other issues, such as the existence of the organisation's own worked out competencies, or the uniqueness of the jobs to be measured. Other factors might be the likelihood of jobs changing, the experience of the organisation in relation to 360-degree feedback, and the demographic relevance of the norm group.

We often advise organisations that are contemplating a large-scale, customised project to start with a proprietary instrument that approximates to their needs. Doing this gets the organisation used to maximising 360-degree feedback. It allows it to withdraw from the experiment without having committed large financial resources, and reveals other decisions to take, such as how to carry out briefing and facilitation. Thus, the implementation of a subsequent customised project becomes easier.

Table 4 opposite summarises the different uses of generic and customised feedback instruments.

Let us assume that you have decided you want your own questionnaire. The time has now come to design it. However, before questions can be written, you need to carry out some preparatory work to lay a firm basis for the questionnaire. In some cases this may already have been done for you. For example, the overall purpose and target population may have been defined, or the organisation may have carried out a competency project as a basis for recruitment or for a performance management system. In other cases no work will have been done; if this is so then you will need to carry out these preparatory steps.

Although Chapter 5 deals more fully with validation, I must emphasise that design and validation go hand in hand. Validation needs to take place throughout the history of a 360-degree feedback instrument.

Table 4

GENERIC V CUSTOMISED 360-DEGREE FEEDBACK

Circumstances	Proprietary	Customised
Emphasis on 'usual' management competencies	✓	✓
Emphasis on interactive skills	✓	✓
Large-scale operation	✓	✓
Small-scale operation	✓	
Need to experiment, pilot	✓	
Need to sell the concept	✓	
Unique/different jobs		✓
Jobs subject to change		✓
Organisation's own competencies		✓
Norm group not relevant		✓

Specification

There are many questions to ask and to answer at this stage of the instrument's design. All of these questions relate to the eventual validity of the whole. It is recommended that the answers to these questions are documented, as they will serve to remind future users of the intended purpose of the instrument, and will help to ensure that it is used within its scope.

☐ What is the overall objective?
☐ What are the specific objectives?
☐ Are there other layers of objectives?

Chapter 3 describes the main uses of 360-degree feedback. However, you may need to analyse these further, bringing you to more specific aims such as:

☐ the need to achieve cultural change in the organisation, moving from results-orientation to an orientation on results through people
☐ the encouragement of self-development by individuals

- ☐ the improvement of the standard of management throughout the organisation
- ☐ increased organisational knowledge about the way that different groups of managers are rated
- ☐ the definition of particular development needs that exist across the population.

You will also need to consider:

- ☐ What is the intended population?
- ☐ Who will the participants be?
- ☐ Who will the respondents be?
- ☐ What are the main (relevant) characteristics of the respondents?

You might intend the instrument to cover the entire management population of the company, eg about 500 employees at senior management, middle management and supervisory levels. The respondents might be self, boss, direct reports and (where relevant) second-level reports. They may cover a broad range of people, from highly educated professionals, to office juniors and shop-floor workers.

All respondents may not be familiar with the culture change initiative which is described in detail in their company's communication documents. This could include behavioural descriptions of the company's vision of the manager of the future.

What demographic questions will we need to ask participants, in order to get meaningful strategic information later about different groups within the organisation? We may want to know their management level, their gender, their age, and their number of years' of service in the organisation.

There is more to questionnaire design than questionnaire design! You will also be designing the accompanying administrative documents and planning how to introduce the process. Because of this it is a good idea at this early stage of the project to inform yourself about some wider issues in the organisation; for example:

- ☐ What are the style and culture of the organisation?
- ☐ How advanced is it technologically, for example in terms of personal computers?

- ☐ What previous experience of 360-degree feedback exists?
- ☐ What is its reception likely to be?
- ☐ What other measures of performance exist?
- ☐ Are there any human resources systems with which the 360-degree measurement needs to be compatible?

The organisation may already have an open culture and have experienced 360-degree feedback. There may already be a competency model and a performance management system within which you want the new process to rest. The workforce may consist of highly qualified people, but may be located in two countries which have quite different cultures.

Design: establish content domain

We start with a job analysis in order to ensure that the final instrument measures the factors that are most important to job performance. It is easy to take a short cut at this stage of the process. This would be unfortunate, as it is an essential activity to ensure that the right factors are being measured.

In practical terms, we need to establish what activities the effective participant should perform in order to design the items for the questionnaire. One of the benefits of carrying out this work is that the results are likely also to be of interest to others in the organisation. Remuneration, training, performance appraisal, and selection are just a few of the other activities that should start with a job analysis.

A job analysis is a 'systematic process for collecting information on the important work-related aspects of a job' (Gatewood and Feild, 1994). It can be focused on different types of work-related information such as:

- ☐ the work activities or tasks that the participant is required to perform in order to meet specific objectives, and how these tasks fit together
- ☐ the prerequisites (in terms of personal characteristics) that enable the participant to perform their job
- ☐ the tools, equipment and environment of the participant that enable or impede them in their work.

For the purpose of 360-degree feedback, the focus of the job analysis should be on the activities or tasks that enable the participant to achieve their work objectives. Some of the techniques that provide a greater understanding of these features of the participant's job are briefly described below. For a more comprehensive discussion of the issues and techniques of job analysis, refer to Pearn and Kandola's comprehensive Manager's Guide.

Observation

This method is applicable to many different types of work. At its most simple, it involves the observer viewing the work that the participant is performing, and taking some specific notes about the activities seen. This is useful to give an overview of the role of the participant. The simple observation can be combined with an interview, either during or after the observation, so that the observer can clarify or get further information about any observation made. Behavioural observation is a more specific technique, which focuses upon the behaviour of the participant, rather than on the tasks they must carry out, or on their goals.

Self-description

This method relies on the participant to give an oral or written description of their job. These self-descriptions can take the form of a report, a diary or work-log, or an interview where the participant is asked to describe a 'typical day'. The narrative is then analysed for the important behaviours, which can involve making inferences or drawing on other information about how the tasks that are described are achieved. The advantage of the written method is that the analyst does not need to be present. The advantage of the interview method is that the interviewer can control the level of detail or the focus of the description.

Interviews

Interviews are a part of many different techniques, but can also be used specifically on their own. Interviews involve an analyst asking questions of the participant with the aim of yielding information about the behaviours important to their job. They can be unstructured or structured, and can be applied to any existing job. Recording information, while composing and asking questions that probe further, while retaining the trust and interest of the participant and steering the interview to cover all relevant areas, is difficult. The degree of the analyst's skill is likely to be the major factor in how useful an unstructured interview might be. For less experienced interviewers it is best to structure the interview carefully beforehand.

Co-counselling

Two job-holders are brought together to interview each other about their jobs. The outcome can vary, depending on their interviewing skills, the briefing they are given, and on how free they feel to talk with each other.

Critical incident

This technique helps an interviewer to determine the elements of job performance that make a difference in certain critical situations. First the interviewee is asked to identify an incident where a job holder performed particularly well, and where their performance was the critical factor in determining the successful outcome. Then they are asked to describe in detail the incident, the background, and what the job holder actually did. This procedure is not designed to produce an exhaustive list of important behaviours, but rather will add to information gathered using other methods.

Repertory grid

The repertory grid technique gets at the personal constructs by which an interviewee categorises how different job holders perform the same job differently. The job holders are organised into 'triads', two of whom are good at their job, and one who is less good. The interviewee is asked what the two good job holders have in common that makes them different from the third job holder. When the interviewee replies, naming a construct, the interviewer probes for more detail by asking how the interviewee can tell that a person is good or bad on the construct. This technique is flexible and produces useful, descriptive information, but again, it will not produce an exhaustive list.

Structured job analysis techniques

These are formal data gathering techniques that are backed up by the materials and forms required, and by computer-based systems that aid the analysis of the information. Examples would be *'Position Analysis' Questionnaire* (available from Oxford Psychologists' Press) and *Work Profiling System* (available from Saville and Holdsworth Ltd).

A combination of two or more of these techniques is often the best approach.

It is worth mentioning here the legal benefits of carrying out a job analysis as part of questionnaire design and validation. McEvoy and Beck-Dudley (in Gatewood and Feild, 1994) conducted a survey between 1979 and 1990 of US Federal appeals courts on the discrimination cases relating to appraisal systems. They categorised the cases on the basis of outcome and found that there were four characteristics of appraisal systems that were significantly related to the outcome. All of these have implications for 360-degree feedback. In the eyes of the law, some protection to the organisation is afforded by appraisal systems that are based upon a job analysis, are behavioural, where evaluators are given specific instructions and where the appraisal results are reviewed with the employees. While the UK is not presently as litigious as the USA, it pays to be prepared!

The analysis techniques that I have described will lead to the establishment of the factors considered to be the most important to job performance. The factors will take the form of competencies, performance definitions, or behavioural statements, which will form the basic architecture of the questionnaire. An example of a list of competencies and definitions appears in Table 5.

As mentioned earlier, you could find yourself presented with a ready-made list of competencies developed for another project. This should save you from having to repeat any job analysis work. However, if you do receive such a list it is good practice to ask how the originators arrived at it. A two-hour session as part of a senior management conference is not usually the best way to research, analyse, define and describe a comprehensive series of such statements.

The list of headings and competencies shown in Table 5 was part of a much longer list developed from some work a com-

Table 5

COMPETENCY HEADINGS AND DEFINITIONS

Competency heading	Definition
Personal integrity	The ability to gain the trust and confidence of others interacting in a fair and honest manner
Decisiveness	The willingness to reach a decision using the available information
Proactivity and forward thinking	The ability to think ahead, influence events, and take initiatives
Team leadership	The ability to obtain quality outputs
Vision	The ability to describe an ideal state or condition, and align others towards its accomplishments
Communicating	The ability to listen to others and express oneself clearly
Quality of results	The commitment to produce high quality work consistently over time
Business knowledge and sense	The ability to understand general business principles and practices, and perceive issues in financial and commercial terms
Empowerment	The willingness to create a work environment in which people are encouraged to develop their full potential
Motivating	The ability to create a satisfying work environment which encourages others to work towards group goals
Problem-solving	The ability to analyse complex information to solve problems which arise in the performance of work roles

pany carried out to develop its corporate values and beliefs. The statement of values contained such concepts as results orientation, professionalism, recognition, empowerment and teamworking. The longer list of competencies aimed to describe in general terms what managers would be doing if they were 'living' these beliefs.

Some questionnaires stop at this point and ask respondents to rate only the competencies. This has the advantage of being short and easily administered. Unfortunately, it is not to be recommended. The reason is that the feedback would still leave too many vague areas or unanswered questions. The fundamental purpose of operating 360-degree feedback is not simply to provide feedback! It is to change behaviour. Unless its generation and communication achieve this then you are left with an interesting exercise, the response to which is 'So what?' For example, look at this competency:

Diversity
'The willingness to work with individuals and integrate the differences that exist among others'.

There could be as many as 30 individual skills or behaviours that go to make up this competency. So if someone rates it as ineffective, which of the desired behaviours did they have in mind? There are not enough clues in the feedback to help the participant improve or develop their performance.

Competencies are nevertheless a very useful ingredient of the questionnaire. They provide a model that describes the general content domain. They provide a base on which to build detailed questions. Also, if they are included in the questionnaire and assessed for their importance to the participant's job, they can then help to indicate priority areas for attention. For example, let us say that in the list in Table 5 my respondents rate team leadership as of high importance, but problem-solving as of lesser importance in my job. If the detailed questions then reveal that my skills are lacking in both areas I can put the team leadership skills ahead of the problem-solving ones on my personal development plan, because they are more key to my job.

Large amounts of detailed data can result from 360-degree feedback. Helping the participant to prioritise therefore becomes critical. Competencies used in the way I have described can do much to assist this process.

Decide the level of specificity of items
Although some 360-degree feedback systems rely solely on open-ended questions in which respondents can say whatever

they want, most questionnaires are built around rated questions (or 'items') which respondents are asked to rate on a scale. We will talk about scales later, but for now let us concentrate on the questions themselves. An item describes behaviour; it is a statement of what the participant does or says; it shows how they are acting to demonstrate an aspect of the competency.

For example, the competency *communicating* is a basket of behaviours such as:

☐ listening
☐ writing
☐ speaking
☐ reacting.

These in turn can be broken into more detail. For example, to demonstrate 'listening' a person may be:

☐ using appropriate body language, like nodding
☐ asking questions
☐ summarising what you say
☐ letting you finish.

We can go further. To demonstrate 'appropriate body language' a person may be:

☐ facing you while you are talking
☐ looking you in the eye
☐ keeping still
☐ leaning forward
☐ nodding
☐ grunting their agreement!

What we have here is therefore a hierarchy of behaviour with the most general at the top and the most detailed at the bottom. This is illustrated in Figure 4.

The skill of the item writer is in selecting the most appropriate level at which to pitch the question. This involves being able to describe behaviour in a very detailed way. It also involves knowing how to make the right trade-offs between minute description, with the masses of detail that entails, and more

Figure 4

A HIERARCHY OF BEHAVIOUR

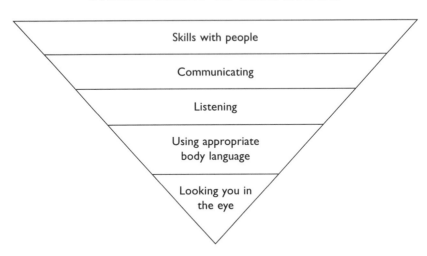

general, but practical, ways of encapsulating the behaviours which go to make up a job.

Here are some tips on item writing, which experience and research have told us help to make questions clear and answerable.

Design the item pool

Begin each sentence with a verb

The best 360-degree questions are those which describe behaviour. For our purposes, behaviour is what people do or say. It is not how they feel, what their outlook is, or what they are like as a person; it is not who they are, but what they do. Items should therefore describe some activity that the respondent can either see or hear in their relationship with the participant. Remember the tip of the iceberg mentioned in Chapter 1 (page 11).

I tend to avoid the passive voice, eg 'is seen by others ...' Also, verbs such as 'is', 'has' and 'can' are not really active enough.

For example, the statement 'Has a keen outlook' is trying to describe a person's attitude rather than what they do. This could be revised to: 'Approaches difficult work issues with enthusiasm.' Such a statement is much more behavioural, and therefore easier for the respondent to recall.

Length of item

A useful target is to make the sentence between five and ten words long. If it is much shorter than this it may be too terse to be understandable; much longer and you may be trying to express more than one thought.

For example, the statement 'Shows discretion' is not very specific. Ask yourself 'What will this person be doing when showing discretion?' The question might result in a statement like: 'Maintains confidentiality when dealing with sensitive issues', ie it is much more specific.

Describe one behaviour at a time

The respondents will have to rate the behaviour on a simple scale. This can make for ease of answering but it is also very restrictive. The respondent has no freedom to express doubt or to hedge their bets. If the item contains two or more different thoughts, therefore, to which one does the answer refer? Or is it both?

This is a common mistake and one into which item writers can easily slip without realising it. Thus, 'Gives personal performance feedback to staff in a timely, sensitive fashion' covers two ideas: timely and sensitive. These are quite different concepts, each of which probably deserves its own question:

'Gives performance feedback at the appropriate time'

'Gives their views on your performance in a sensitive way.'

Beware of using 'and' or 'or'

These words can also indicate the presence of two thoughts. If you use 'and' to connect two words of different meaning, for example 'speaks clearly and politely' or 'readily acts as a mentor to staff and peers', what happens if the respondent thinks the participant speaks clearly but not politely, or mentors staff but not peers?

Arguably, close synonyms are less serious and can even develop the meaning when one word is insufficient. For example 'Inspires the trust and confidence of others'. Trust and confidence have slightly different meanings, but not so different that they cannot be linked; one develops the other. However, in 'Praise and recognise others for high quality performance' is there any difference between 'giving praise' and 'recognising others' when it comes to high performance? Probably not. So why use two repetitive expressions where one will suffice? Effectively written items are those which use language precisely and economically.

Use everyday language

Remember the people who will be answering the questions. Make sure that your language is meaningful to all parties concerned. For example, if you were asking people to assess the customer service skills of a medical practice receptionist via the self, the doctor and the patients, which of these questions would you use?

'Maximises the practice's reputation for effective responses to patient enquiries'

This might be understandable by the self and the doctor, but to patients it may be less clear than saying:

'Makes patients feel happy with the way their enquiries are handled'

I am not suggesting that all questions should be written in words of less than three syllables! I am suggesting that the language used should be appropriate to the participants and respondents.

Minimise judgmental expressions

The use of words like 'well', 'excellent', and 'effective' are sometimes unavoidable, but can be unnecessary and confusing. Thus, in 'Makes effective formal presentations', what does 'effective' mean? Clear? Convincing? Interesting? Not too long? Remember, the participant may have to act on this feedback. Adjectives should add meaning, not cover it up.

Address the reader

Sometimes it is helpful to address the reader personally. Thus, 'Allows you to speak without interrupting' encourages the respondent to focus on their personal, direct relationship with the participant.

Relate to the competency or value

Competencies or skill categories often form the basis of 360-degree feedback questionnaires. It is important, therefore, to make sure that the items you devise relate demonstrably to the competency they are trying to cover.

Use 'demonstrate' or 'show' sparingly

As we have seen, an item is a behavioural statement that describes how the person is demonstrating a competency. Sometimes we can be genuinely at a loss to know how to frame a statement. In other words, we cannot think of a way of describing behaviour that does its job of demonstrating a level of performance or competence. In these cases we can then write the item like this: 'Demonstrates the ability to think on his or her feet', or 'Shows the capacity for conceptual thought'. It is fine to do this occasionally, but it can be overdone, when it becomes a substitute for thinking behaviours through. There is usually a better solution, so do not take the 'show/demonstrate' way out all the time.

Finally, here is a list of items which contain some of the faults referred to above. Try to rephrase them and check your answers with our version at the end of this chapter (page 94).

1   Has an engaging personality
2   Asked by others for advice
3   Understands the importance of the difference between cause and effect
4   Willingly takes an unpopular stand on issues about which he or she has convictions and where there is a need to question the *status quo*
5   Maximises available opportunities in others for learning, development, and growth
6   Demonstrates effective communication techniques.

Decide the number of items

Questionnaire lengths vary tremendously. I have seen questionnaires ranging from 10 items to 200. Clearly, the longer the questionnaire the more information becomes available for the participant. However, at a certain point the detail can become counterproductive. It gets too much for the respondents and participants to cope with, and leads to an adverse reaction on their part.

Consider how many items of information result from a 10-competency, 100-item questionnaire, using two scales (see the following section on scales) and asking for feedback from self, boss, five reports, peers, and internal customers (ie, five respondent groups totalling 17 people), and with four open-ended questions.

The participant would then be confronted with a feedback report which contains 3,060 pieces of numerical or graphical data plus 68 sentences to read. They also have to look at the differences between the self scores and those of the other raters. Having read it they then have to prioritise it! And don't forget the total time (let us say 45 minutes each) for each person to complete it – almost 13.5 man hours!

This example in Table 6 below is not particularly extreme. It shows how the amount of data can proliferate to unmanageable lengths together with the amount of time needed for questionnaire completion.

Some organisations and suppliers sincerely believe in the value of such complex, rigorous instruments. They clearly see the benefits of extensive analysis as being worth the cost in time and money. However, as this technique gains acceptance throughout organisations then the use of the longer type of questionnaire will probably diminish. It is my belief, based on experience with many organisations, that most 360-degree

Table 6

'BITS' OF DATA IN A 360-DEGREE FEEDBACK QUESTIONNAIRE

10 competencies x 3 (current v expected plus gap size) =	30 bits	
30 bits shown first graphically and then numerically (x 2) =		*60 bits*
100 items x 3 (current v expected plus gap size) =	300 bits	
300 bits x 5 respondent groups =	1,500 bits	
1,500 bits shown both graphically and numerically x 2 =		*3,000 bits*
Total		**3,060 bits**
Four open-ended questions x 17 people = 68 sentences		

feedback questionnaires need contain only 25–70 questions. This is usually enough to provide people with adequate amounts of data on which to plan their development.

Whatever the intended final number of questions, it is a good idea to develop an item pool of at least 25 per cent more items than are required. It is important to start with too many items, as you will be removing some 'bad' items during validation in order to improve the quality of the instrument.

Design scales

Several scales can be used for rated questions.

Frequency

This is probably the least judgemental type of scale because it asks the respondent merely to state how often they see a participant behaviour being used, eg:

1   Almost never
2   Sometimes
3   Generally
4   Almost always
5   Always

My earlier comment about not using value-laden words like 'excellent' in the item does not apply here. Items usually need a quality or value element in the question when attached to frequency scales. See for example Table 7.

Table 7

QUESTIONS CONTAINING VALUES

	Always				
	Almost always				
	Generally				
	Sometimes				
	Almost never				
Quickly gain insights into complex problems?	①	②	③	④	⑤
Answer questions in specific detail?	①	②	③	④	⑤
Negotiate differences of opinion fairly?	①	②	③	④	⑤

So, with a frequency scale the issue is how often a desirable behaviour is observed. This makes the feedback less emotional because the respondent merely has to record the number of times they see a behaviour occur, rather than state how good or bad they think it is.

Effectiveness

As the name implies, effectiveness scales ask for an opinion from the respondent on the skill or quality with which an activity is carried out, eg:

1   This behaviour needs to be addressed urgently
2   In need of development
3   Performance could be better
4   Without noticeable strengths or weaknesses
5   A genuine strength
6   Supremely effective

Importance

Importance scales are sometimes used on their own. Sometimes they are used in combination with another scale. In both cases they are very useful because they help to set priorities for change and improvement, eg:

1   Extremely important
2   Very important
3   Important
4   Somewhat important
5   Not important

Agreement

Sometimes the respondent can be asked to state the extent to which they agree with a series of statements about the participant's performance, eg:

1   Strongly agree
2   Agree
3   Neither agree nor disagree
4   Disagree
5   Strongly disagree

Dual scales

Some of these scales, when used in combination, can provide more powerful and detailed feedback to the participant. For example, current and expected frequency tells the participant not only how often they do something, but also how often they ought to be doing something. When a gap appears between the two scores then the participant knows either that they are not doing enough of a particular behaviour, or too much. See figure 5 for example.

The example in Figure 6 links effectiveness with the importance of a particular behaviour. Ineffective behaviours of lesser importance can be left until those of greater importance have been addressed.

Scale lengths

The number of points on a scale in 360-degree feedback questionnaires can vary from four to ten. Opinions seem to vary about the best length, with some saying that ten points allow people proper freedom to differentiate, and others saying that five points is perfectly adequate for this purpose. Having too few points removes the opportunity to express nuances, and can therefore produce invalid answers. Too many points could be asking people to express nuances which are beyond them – with the same result.

As we have seen already, there are several types of descriptors available. The examples just listed show the most frequently used scale descriptors.

We have found from experience that it is a good idea to include a specific place for respondents to mark if they cannot answer a question.

Odd or even?

Questionnaire designers also have to take a decision on whether to make the elements in a scale an odd or even number. The argument against an odd number is that it can enable people to take refuge in a 'middle of the road' comment if they do not want to commit themselves on a particular item. Some respondents who are not sure whether they are able to answer they might also be tempted to play safe and take the middle ground. The argument for an even number is that the scale can force the

Figure 5

CURRENT V EXPECTED

Current Performance
How often does this occur? (Choose One)

Your Expectations
How often should this occur? (Choose One)

To what extent does this person ...

	Almost Never	Sometimes	Generally Almost Always	Always		Almost Never	Sometimes	Generally Almost Always	Always
1 Share technical expertise with you/others?	① ②	③	④	⑤		① ②	③	④	⑤
2 Express his/her point of view in a tactful way	① ②	③	④	⑤		① ②	③	④	⑤

Figure 6

EFFECTIVENESS V IMPORTANCE

Effectiveness

Importance

How would you rate the following behaviours in this person ...

	Addressed urgently	Need for development	No strength/weakness	Genuine strength	Supremely effective		Not important	Somewhat important	Important	Very important	Extremely important
1 Lets people know what is expected of them	① ②	③	④	⑤		① ②	③	④	⑤
2 Finds opportunities to carry out one-to-one coaching	① ②	③	④	⑤		① ②	③	④	⑤

respondent away from the middle ground and therefore provide more useful and less bland information. The argument against an even number is that you are removing the opportunity for people who genuinely wish to express the middle ground in their answers. Such people may not appreciate being forced one way or the other and will give what they regard as a wrong answer, or no answer at all.

The arguments about length of scale and whether to have odd or even numbers become somewhat less important in 360-degree feedback because of its multi-rater aspect. The result of a self-assessment, or indeed of an averaged assessment by one group, is a single figure, or a single line on a bar chart. However, with multi-rater assessment there are several figures and several bars, enabling comparisons to be made. Whatever scale is used the differences between the views of the various respondent groups become readily apparent.

In practice, clear feedback results depend much more on the way people are briefed (orally or as part of the questionnaire itself), the header for the items, the clarity of the items themselves, and the appropriateness of the descriptors.

A final point on questionnaire design: it is not just the clarity of the individual parts of the form which is important. These parts have to be consistent with each other. Look again at Figure 5. This question is all about frequency, and all the parts hang together well. In other words the header asks for the 'extent'. It could also ask 'how often' or 'how frequently'. The body of the item agrees with the construction of the header, ie 'share' rather than 'shares'.

The scale also agrees with the header, ie 'almost never–always'. You have only to get one of these parts wrong to produce confusion. How clear is the question in Figure 7?

Having said all that, in my experience most organisations tend to favour a six or ten point scale for a single-scale instrument, and a five point scale for dual.

Design open-ended questions

Rated questions are a key part of the feedback process. They impose a structure on respondents which makes it possible to compare participants' results, and, to compare what different groups of respondents think. They also help the designer to

Figure 7

INCONSISTENCY BETWEEN THE COMPONENTS OF A QUESTION

How often does this person …

I Develops plans for teaching goals · · · · · · · · · · · · · · · ·

Effectiveness

① ② ③ ④ ⑤
1 2 3 4 5

Addressed urgently
Need for development
No strength/weakness
Genuine strength
Supremely effective

Importance

① ② ③ ④ ⑤
1 2 3 4 5

Not important
Somewhat important
Important
Very important
Extremely important

make sure that the competencies and skill categories under examination are properly covered. The resulting data can be scanned or hand-entered, computer scored and processed, and displayed in various compelling graphical formats. The behavioural nature of the items and the graphical presentation encourage a less emotional response from the participant – but not always. For example, here is the response I had recently from a senior manager when first confronted by his feedback:

> Thank you for the report. I am surprised by many of the findings. I do not agree with them because I prefer to think that 25 years of experience, achievement and promotion tell me more than a set of coloured charts.

Respondents can find an exclusive concentration on rated questions too restrictive. Open-ended questions help respondents to use their own words, give examples, and generally put more flesh on to the statistical bones. Such questions usually ask for examples of behaviours that appear particularly effective or ineffective. However, the choice of words is very important to ensure that the feedback is accepted.

Here are some examples from a career development 360-degree feedback questionnaire:

☐ Describe the main strengths in this person's current performance.

☐ Describe what you would see as areas for improvement.

☐ What opportunities would you see facing this person as far as career choice and development are concerned?

☐ What do you see are the main barriers to this person's career development?

Design administrative documents

Many 360-degree feedback projects can run into trouble because of poor communication. This can include unclear instructions, so let us look at the administrative tasks that are closely linked to the questionnaire itself. Writing the instructions for distributing and completing the questionnaire requires just as much skill and attention to detail as devising the items themselves.

Here are some rules which should bring a wry smile to the lips of anyone who has administered a 360-degree feedback project (shades of Murphy's Law):

☐ If someone can forget to put their name on a questionnaire, they will.
☐ If someone can misunderstand what the scales mean, they will.
☐ If you say to someone that the minimum number of raters is four in any group, they will give three.
☐ If you ask for the questionnaire to be completed in pencil they will complete it in ink.
☐ If you ask for it to be returned by a certain date, it won't be.

The main additional items that need to accompany a questionnaire appear below.

Communication to participants
☐ An explanation of the purpose of the project
☐ What the information will be used for
☐ How to choose respondents
☐ How to approach them
☐ Timescales.

A sample instruction sheet is shown in Appendix A.

Instructions for completing the questionnaire
Busy people do not always read the instructions but instead go straight to the task of answering the questions – and get them wrong. Your instructions need to be as clear and detailed as possible without taxing the patience of the reader. In our experience too much detail is better than too little. It is better to be as explicit as possible. Appendix B shows the instructions included in the form. It is also important for participants to have someone independent to contact in case of enquiries.

Some organisations put the onus for managing the return of completed questionnaires in the hands of the participant. This delegation of responsibility makes the administration of the project much easier. It also reinforces the notion that feedback is the responsibility of the participant – not of the department organising the project. Chasing stragglers produces a better rate of completion. However, some organisations do not do this, arguing that questionnaire completion should be voluntary and that chasing up people is coercive, even if they have agreed to participate in the first place. Appendix C shows the front page of a questionnaire, which can also be used by participants or the organisation for tracking purposes.

Communication to respondents

Clarity of communication applies as much to respondents as to participants. As an example, see Appendix D.

Check-list on questionnaire specification

☐ What are the overall objectives?
☐ What are the specific objectives?
☐ Are there any other sub-objectives?
☐ Who are the target population?
☐ How many participants?
☐ Who will be the respondents?
☐ How many respondents?
☐ What demographic data do I want to gather?
☐ What is the style and culture of the organisation?
☐ How technologically advanced is the organisation?
☐ What previous experiences of 360-degree feedback exist?
☐ What will be its likely reception?
☐ What other ways of measuring performance exist?
☐ Is the feedback to link in with other HR processes?

Check-list to establish content domain

☐ Are competencies or other categories available?
☐ If so, what do I need to do to verify them?
☐ If not, what techniques should I use to establish content domain?

Check-list on questionnaire design

Have I:

- ☐ begun each sentence with a verb
- ☐ achieved the right item length
- ☐ described one behaviour at a time
- ☐ used 'and' or 'or' carefully
- ☐ used appropriate language
- ☐ minimised judgmental expressions
- ☐ addressed the reader (if necessary)
- ☐ related items to competencies
- ☐ used 'demonstrate' and 'show' sparingly?

- ☐ What is the most appropriate scale length?
- ☐ What descriptors do I need?
- ☐ Have I matched header, items, and scale?
- ☐ Do I need open-ended questions?

Check-list for administrative items

Have I prepared:

- ☐ a communication to participants
- ☐ instructions for completing the questionnaires
- ☐ a tracking sheet
- ☐ communication to respondents?

'Right' answers to the exercise on page 83

1   Use of 'has'. How does he demonstrate this?
Try: Makes a good first impression on people he or she meets.
2   This is passive.
Try: Readily provides advice to others.
3   'Understands'. How does the participant demonstrate this?
Try: Deals with the causes of problems rather than the symptoms.
4   Two distinct thoughts and quite wordy.
Try: a. Readily takes an unpopular stand on important matters.
      b. Challenges the assumptions behind the *status quo*.

5   I am not sure what this means either! It may not be everyday language.
Try: Encourages others to develop themselves.
6   Could mean any one of dozens of behaviours.
Try: Presents ideas in a persuasive manner.

Reference

GATEWOOD, R. D. *and* FEILD, H. S. (1994) *Human Resource Selection*. 3rd edn, London, Harcourt Brace & Company.

5

VALIDATION AND PILOTING

It is better to solve problems on the basis of data and evidence than on speculation or the past.

Pearn and Kandola

Key points

> □ Validation is the process of gathering evidence that a 360-degree feedback process does what it is designed to do.
> □ It can be divided into issues of reliability, and content, construct, and concurrent validity.
> □ Utility, ie cost effectiveness, is also related to validity.
> □ Validation should take place at each stage of the design cycle, rather than at just one point.
> □ Proper validation makes 360-degree feedback easier to justify internally and defend externally.
> □ Some organisations are unwilling to invest in rigorous validation.

In the case in Table 8, validation and piloting have not been properly carried out on the instrument, and problems that affect the reliability and validity have not been picked up. The questions that Janet is left asking are:
Is the feedback consistent?

□ Did each question create a shared mental picture in my peers?
□ Are the instructions clear?

Do my scores reflect what respondents really think about my behaviour?

□ Does the scale distort people's real views?

Table 8

JANET'S FEEDBACK

It is appraisal time for Janet, a business development manager in the retail sector. She has sent out 360-degree feedback questionnaires to her boss, her staff and her peers. She receives the feedback during a one-to-one session with a facilitator and accepts that there are certain areas for her to develop. She writes down her initial thoughts about what she can do differently, but decides that she needs to clarify further some areas with her peers.

When she sits down with them to discuss her feedback she discovers that many of the questions were ambiguous, so that her peers had very different mental pictures created by the same question. She also discovers that one of her respondents did not feel able to answer some of the questions; but as the instructions were unclear, where she was unable to make a rating she had given her a 6, instead of leaving the question blank. Her peers expressed some concern that the questionnaire did not allow them to give her feedback on her business awareness, which they felt was the single most important area of her job.

Janet then went to talk to her staff, to ask them how they found the questionnaire. Two of them told her that they thought that her boss would be able to identify what they had said. They didn't want to look like whiners, and as they thought that it was compulsory to take part they rated her as they thought her boss would like to see her rated.

Janet is now reviewing her action plan. She really wants to improve, but understandably she does not want to use the feedback report as a basis for prioritisation. She feels she is back at square one.

☐ Do people feel comfortable enough to use the instrument frankly?

Is the feedback a valid representation of my performance on the job?

☐ Does the instrument cover everything that it should?
☐ Does the instrument cover anything that it shouldn't?

Did the company waste money on the development of this instrument?

Validation should answer these questions. It is the process of gathering evidence that a 360-degree feedback process does what it is designed to do. It is also concerned with the ability of an instrument to deliver benefits to the user. Validation is essential for making decisions about how good a 360-degree feedback instrument is. The validation process is generally carried out through 'piloting', ie using the instrument with a sample of the people for whom it is designed, and investigating its success. Piloting is a necessary part of validation. It means that the instrument is evaluated in the context of the specific way that it is going to be used, rather than in a vacuum.

The validation evidence that is collected is generally a mixture of qualitative and quantitative data, and relates to issues of reliability, validity and utility. These issues are described in detail in this chapter.

Reliability

Reliability is the ability of an assessment method to measure consistently and accurately; that is, its ability to reflect 'the truth'. These two features of reliability: accuracy and consistency, are major factors in determining the validity of an instrument. However, they are traditionally dealt with separately, for practical reasons which we will see later. *Accuracy* is the ability of a 360-degree feedback instrument to pinpoint exactly how well a subject performs important aspects of their work. *Consistency* is concerned with the ability of a 360-degree feedback instrument to return the same results if measuring the same thing.

☐ Did each question create a shared mental picture in my respondents?

☐ Are the instructions clear?

☐ Were respondents clear about how to use the rating scale?

☐ Were respondents clear about what to do if they felt unable to answer?

If an instrument is not accurate and consistent it cannot be valid. The threat to reliability that is focused on during the validation of 360-degree feedback instruments is the measurement error. Other sources of unreliability are largely out of our control or are part of the context of the 360-degree feedback process.

Unreliability is visible through fluctuations in scores, and by scores not reflecting what is known from other measures.

However, there are at least three possible sources of variations in 360-degree feedback measurement:

- □ *Human factors*: either brief fluctuations caused by moods, or physical well-being, etc, or longer-term, more stable changes, motivation, attitudes, or increased skills, generally known as growth.
- □ *Contextual changes*: organisational, department or other environmental events or distractions occurring at the time of the measurement.
- □ *Measurement error*: scores do not reflect 'the truth' due to the way the assessment was administered or due to ambiguous or irrelevant questions, unclear instructions or difficulties with the scale.

The relative proportions of the different factors can be influenced to some extent by careful design. It is important, for example, to have an adequate protocol for briefing the participants and respondents, so that differences in the process are kept to a minimum.

When designing and implementing a 360-degree feedback instrument we have some degree of control over the measurement error, and through the use of pilot studies we aim to eliminate the fluctuations in scores that are due to measurement error. Ideally our measurements will reflect the longer term changes in human factors, allowing us to track growth, without being adversely affected by more unstable human factors.

As the measurement is of on-the-job performance, we would expect the context to affect scores to some extent, but as this is not the focus of our measurement, we would not expect it to be the primary source of variation in scores. In practice, eliminating all unwanted sources of variation is an impossible objective. Minimising the effect of these sources on our instrument is the best that we can do.

Validity

Validity is about whether an instrument accurately measures what it is supposed to, and whether its use is relevant to the situation. Validity can be divided into sub-issues. Remember, however, that these aspects of validity are inextricably linked to each other.

Reliability

As already discussed above, reliability contributes to validity.

Content validity

This is the ability of the instrument to cover the appropriate domain.

☐ Does the assessment look at everything that it should?
☐ Does it include anything that it should not cover?
☐ Are the factors covered the ones that really make a difference to participants' work?

In the case of 360-degree feedback used for performance appraisal, it is important that we measure the behaviours and skills that are important to the achievement of work objectives. Where 360-degree feedback is being used as preparation for a course, the content should be relevant to the course coverage. Where 360-degree feedback is being considered as a determinant of pay, the organisation should be certain that it is measuring all the behaviours that it wishes to encourage, and not the behaviours that it wishes to eliminate.

Construct validity

This covers the ability of the instrument to measure a particular theoretical concept.

☐ If scores are supposed to represent a person's performance on a particular theoretical construct, how well do they do so?

Some 360-degree feedback instruments are based upon theoretical research into the behaviours required to be effective in a particular role, for example leadership. It is important to ensure that there is a stable concept or characteristic being measured, and that it is relevant to the individual's job performance. Construct validation tests our hypothesis that what we are measuring is linked to job performance in that construct.

Concurrent validity

This covers the ability of the instrument to measure performance accurately.

☐ Do scores on the 360-degree feedback instrument reflect other objective measurements of the performance?

For this stage of validation our aim is to prove that our instrument measures the behaviours and skills that are important determinants of job performance, so we select another measure of performance that we know to be satisfactory, and compare the measurements.

There is some debate about whether this is useful. The whole point of 360-degree feedback is that it is a better way of evaluating performance than any previous appraisal type. Does it help us, then, to find out whether scores on our new method correlate with scores using previous methods? This argument suggests that previous methods have no validity whatsoever, which is unlikely to be true. It is sometimes possible to look for direct indicators of results to compare with 360-degree scores. Finding a useful criterion of performance remains the single biggest difficulty in assessing concurrent validity. This is discussed in some depth under 'Practical steps in validation' (see below).

Utility

Related to validity and reliability is the question of whether a measurement instrument is cost effective. Is the increase in performance yielded by the use of the instrument worth more than the money spent developing and implementing? Does the process add value that is greater than the cost of the instrument?

Practical steps in validation

In order to make this section as practical as possible, I have gone into quite some detail on the methods used, with examples. However, some of the detailed statistical procedures are outside the scope of this book. Where this is the case, I have referred to other texts that cover these. I have already covered defining the purpose, establishing the content domain, and developing the initial item pool as part of the design stage in Chapter 4. Let us assume, therefore, that you have carried out these important steps and now have an initial item pool. The activities that follow complete the validation process.

Examine the item pool

Check that respondents will be able to answer the questions. A focus group, representative of potential respondents is worthwhile to draw attention to any problems with the initial pool in terms of ambiguous questions, unanswerable questions (questions that are jargonistic or that do not relate to behaviours that respondents can observe), double-barrelled questions, verbose questions. Modify or eliminate any items that are found at this stage to be poor.

Ensure complete coverage of content domain

A focus group of respondents can also be used to help you check that the items adequately cover the skill areas identified in the job analysis and that there are no areas that were missed during job analysis which are of high importance to the participants' job role.

Specify the protocol

The protocol is the administration procedure, or the way that you intend the instrument to be used. I referred to its design earlier in Chapter 4. It should be a carefully designed policy, written down formally in the draft manual before the first administration of the 360-degree assessment. As with ability tests, measurement error can result from deviations from this protocol, so it should be given a high priority and importance. When it comes to piloting, the protocol needs to be tested out on participants and respondents alongside the questionnaire itself.

Decide on a criterion

A criterion is an alternative measurement of job performance which is to be used to test the concurrent validity of the instrument. It is best to decide on this before proceeding with the pilot. There are many different job performance measures that can be used singly or in combination as a criterion measure. However, choosing an appropriate criterion and deciding how to collect this data can be extremely obscure and difficult, depending on the nature of the job.

It is worth asking what measures are used for the validation of selection instruments or for training evaluation, and also what measures exist already. If the answer is 'none', then think about how the measures that you decide upon can be put to good use elsewhere.

Three basic types of job performance measures can be used:

Output data, such as the quantity or quality of output. Production data is a useful indicator of work performance since the measurement generally reflects the aspects of output that are most important to the organisation. It is important to remember that the data should reflect *individual* performance rather than group performance, eg in a customer-service role, repeat business or number of referrals may be used.

Personnel data, such as promotions or salary increases. Personnel records are another source of existing data about a participant's performance, but some of the variables measured are more useful than others. Attendance does seem to be a pre-requisite for performance, but will not tell us a great deal about the quality of performance. Promotions may at first seem to be a good criterion, but the limited variation in promotions across a group of participants will lower the validity. Another problem with personnel data is the period of time over which the data is collected; a criterion measure should be 'concurrent' with the 360-degree feedback measure, that is, it should cover the same time period.

Subjective data, such as ratings of job performance. An individual who is familiar with the work of another is required to judge their work. For the purpose of a criterion measurement this should be a single rating that measures overall performance. It can be difficult to decide who is best qualified to make this rating. The entire rationale for using a 360-degree feedback assessment rather than a single boss assessment is that boss ratings reflect only one perspective on a person's performance, and are notoriously unreliable!

Conduct pilot(s)
It is important that the conditions of the pilot reproduce as far as possible the conditions that will exist once the 360-degree feedback process is rolled out. As you are piloting the entire process, and not just the instrument, it is important

that pilot participants should not be given special treatment. Equally, it is important that the feedback form looks realistic, ie the form should be properly desk-top published, replicating the 'skunk' and 'timing' marks that the eventual scannable form will have.

The exception to this is that the participants and respondents should be made aware that the process is new and that they will be asked for their feedback. It is a good idea to ask participants to make notes on any points that they think are particularly good and on any points that they would like to see changed as they notice them. This will help them when you ask for feedback later.

The pilot sample should be large enough to include a representative sample of the different participants in the intended population. Look back at your written notes on the characteristics of the intended population and make sure, for example, that you have covered the different levels of staff. As a rule of thumb, a sample size of about 5 per cent should be adequate. It is recommended that you divide your pilot group into two or more groups so that revisions to the questionnaire and modifications to the process based on the information from the initial pilot can be investigated.

Gather feedback on problems

This is usually done by a combination of questionnaires and focus groups, yielding both quantitative and qualitative data. This feedback will lead you to make changes, both to the questionnaire and to the process. You are likely to discover certain difficulties experienced with particular questions, but this is not a problem as you started with too many questions for this very reason. Try to retain an overview of the domain that you are covering, as deleting several questions in one skill area may leave it with very scant coverage. If you find yourself in this situation, it is advisable that you get your respondents to help you create additional items that will work. Bear in mind that any new items will need to be included in a second pilot.

Prepare final form and manual

The final form of the questionnaire should look similar to the form used for the last pilot. If for any reason it does not, then you should consider carrying out another pilot. It is important that you produce a manual that describes:

- the instrument and why it was produced
- the scope and the intended population
- the specific way that the instrument should be used
- the validation work that you have carried out (specifically, to help with any future replications)
- the validity and utility of the instrument.

If the above steps are *systematically* and *correctly* applied to the design of a new instrument, you can expect that the instrument will achieve a satisfactory level of validity when used for the application and population for which it was intended. The following section further explores the psychometric characteristics of the instrument.

Further validation work

Frequency analysis

- Are the ratings distributed in a 'normal' bell-shaped curve?
- To what extent are the scores skewed?
- Does the curve have a wide or a narrow base?

A frequency analysis of 360-degree feedback involves plotting the mean score given by each respondent to all the pilot group participants on the same graph and examining the distribution of ratings given across the scale. It is generally true that more people perform in an average way than in an extreme way. When you plot the scores of many human performance measures against the frequency of scores occurring, a 'normal' curve is a feature of the distribution seen in Figure 8.

Respondents more often rate people as average, than they rate them at the extremes. For this reason we would expect a curve that looks roughly 'normal'.

However, some 'skew' may be expected and tolerable, ie we expect the average to be above the average that we would get if we plotted the scores for the entire population. Poor performance is eliminated to some extent for two reasons: those who

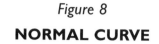

Figure 8

NORMAL CURVE

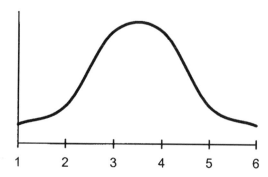

would perform at the bottom of the scale tend to be weeded out by the selection processes, or they tend to move to a different job – people do not like to stay long in positions where they feel they are performing badly. So a distribution curve for a 360-degree questionnaire might look more like Figure 9.

What does it mean if the frequency plot does not look like the examples in Figures 8 and 9?

There is probably a good reason for the difference, and examining your questions, the scale, and the process will enable you to determine where the problem lies. Some factors that will affect the distribution of the scores are:

□ the scale is too extreme
□ too few respondents in the pilot group

Figure 9

SKEW

- [ ] the questions have a very strong positive emphasis
- [ ] the questions have a very strong negative emphasis
- [ ] respondents have little confidence in the confidentiality of the process
- [ ] respondents did not understand the instructions on how to use the scale.

In Figure 10 the width of the distribution is very narrow, suggesting that the questionnaire does not discriminate well between participants. This will make it less useful in some applications, eg as a determinant of performance-based pay. One way to remedy the problem is to make the wording of the scale less extreme, so that respondents are encouraged to make finer distinctions between participants.

You may want to do a frequency analysis that breaks down the rating behaviour of the different groups, but bear in mind that you may need to gather more data before this will yield any useful results.

Item response percentage
Calculate the percentage of the total respondents who answered each question. This can identify two possible causes of problems:

- [ ] If the questionnaire is too long the item response drops off for items towards the end of the questionnaire.

Figure 10

DISTRIBUTION GRAPH

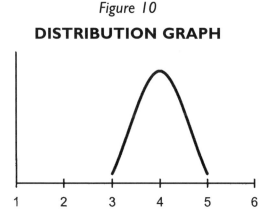

1   2   3   4   5   6

☐ If any question is ambiguous or irrelevant, a lower item response percentage will flag this up from the pilot data.

Intercorrelation of items

Correlate scores for each item with each other item. Very high correlations will indicate items that may be redundant. If questions are rated very similarly by respondents, the length of the questionnaire could usefully be shortened by including only one of the two.

Factor analysis

This section begins with the intercorrelation of items, and 'factors' are identified. The factors are variables made up of different items that explain the variance in scores. This allows you to identify redundant items, and also to structure your feedback under valid factor headings.

Demographic cuts of the data

When you have gathered data from a large enough number of participants, you may wish to look at the data from a strategic viewpoint, to consider differences between different groups of participants and to consider rating behaviour at different levels. For example, are female employees rated higher or lower on average than male employees?

Examine criterion validity

Measurement of the criterion should also have been carried out at about the same period of time as the 360-degree feedback. It is now time to carry out a statistical comparison of the criterion scores and the 360-degree feedback assessment scores.

The particular statistical test of significance of the relationship between the scores collected by the two different methods will depend upon the nature of the criterion. Different statistical tests make different assumptions and it is important to choose the correct type. Remember that the criterion may not be expected to have a linear relationship with the 360-degree feedback scores.

You may wish to get advice on this stage from a statistician or an occupational psychologist in order to ensure that the best use is made of the data that you have so carefully collected. You can also refer to Coolican's (1994) book for further help.

Examine utility

The utility can be estimated by comparing the value of the workforce as it is, with the value of the workforce as it will be when 360-degree feedback has been implemented, and taking away the cost from this estimated increase in value.

Estimate how much improvement will be made through the use of the 360-degree feedback, and what sort of improvement will be made. This information can come from a retest, which should be carried out after a period of about eight months as a minimum. Or, it can come from the job-performance criterion used earlier to assess the criterion validity.

Place a value on the improvement made. This can be extremely difficult. It depends upon the nature of the participants' job and upon the nature of improvements made. You will need to extrapolate to include the rest of the participants. Don't forget indirect improvements of aspects such as:

- the value of mistakes *not* made
- the indirect effects of improvements (eg lower turnover from managers who have become less aggressive in their style)
- reduced stress of participants (eg through greater role clarity)
- increased motivation and improved relationships.

This list is by no means exhaustive. It is best if you ask your participants and respondents to identify the areas and the degree of improvement.

Work out the cost of the process, extrapolating to the rest of the participants, including:

- development costs
- processing and printing costs
- cost of training facilitators
- time spent by participants, respondents, administrators and facilitators in various activities
- cost of follow-up activities.

Take the cost of implementation away from the value of improvements made. This gives you the return on investment, or 'utility' of the instrument.

Establish norms

If you wish to compare participants to the group of which they are a member, then it is important to keep all data that is collected to establish clear norms. It can help participants to see how they are rated as compared to their peer group, or their department. It can also help in establishing changes over time and in looking at the strengths and development needs of a particular group or department.

Evaluation

Finally, I described in Chapter 3 how 360-degree feedback can be used to assess the effectiveness of training and development programmes, particularly in the areas of behaviour and results. Those who wish may also turn the tables, because it is possible to use part of the Kirkpatrick model to evaluate a 360-degree feedback project. Appendix E contains a good example of this, a questionnaire designed by a major 360-degree feedback user as an assessment of reaction. One round of feedback, based on an extensively validated questionnaire, has almost finished – with re-testing starting in a few months' time. As an interim measure, however, they have decided to carry out this survey as a comprehensive means of making the process as effective as possible for next time. The survey consists of two questionnaires, the first aimed at participants and the second at reporting staff who have completed a questionnaire on their manager.

Final thoughts

Having spent this chapter describing what *can* be done to ensure the validity, reliability and utility of 360-degree feedback instruments, I have two 'groans' to express.

In my experience of working with clients to create customised 360-degree feedback instruments, it has proved very difficult to persuade them (with some honourable exceptions) to invest in validation. The minimum of validation work tends to be acceptable to the organisation, but the further validation which will allow an organisation to feel proud and confident in its use of the instrument is rarely considered.

I also have difficulty selling enough education to go with the 360-degree feedback product. It concerns me that many organisations do not understand, or take seriously enough, the importance of the informed, skilled facilitator in determining the success or failure of a 360-degree feedback process. It takes only a couple of bad experiences of an instrument to give it a bad name within an organisation. This can happen through misuse, inappropriate use or unskilled facilitation. It seems a shame that all the work paid for to create a valid, reliable, useful instrument is wasted by the lack of inclination to buy the expertise to use it.

I urge you to go the full distance in validation and we will all sleep better at night!

Validation check-list

☐ Have I/others established the purpose of this feedback project?

☐ What work has been done to establish the content domain?

☐ What further work (if any) do I need to do on the content domain?

☐ Did my initial design allow for 25 per cent more questions than were eventually needed?

☐ What steps did I take to examine the initial time pool?

☐ Have I made sure that no areas were missed?

☐ Have I specified the protocol?

☐ Have I decided on a criterion?

☐ Are my pilot groups representative of the whole population?

☐ Have the pilot groups been properly briefed?

☐ Is the pilot as close to the real thing as possible?

☐ What techniques did I use to gather and analyse feedback from the pilot?

☐ Have I produced the manual?

☐ What further validation work do I want or need to carry out?

References

AIKEN, L. R. (1994) *Psychological Testing and Assessment*. 8th edn, Hemel Hempstead, Allyn and Bacon.

CIPOLLA, L. J. *and* HICKOK, C. W. *A Brief Investigation of the Characteristics, Reliability and Validity of the Leadership Assessment Survey*. Unpublished paper.

COOLICAN, H. (1994) *Research Methods and Statistics in Psychology*. 2nd edn, London, Hodder & Stoughton.

GATEWOOD, R. D. *and* FEILD, H. S. (1994) *Human Resource Selection*. 3rd edn, London, Harcourt Brace & Company.

GOLDSTEIN, I. L. (1992) *Training in Organisations*. 3rd edn, Brooks/Cole Publishing Company.

PEARN, M. *and* KANDOLA, R. (1993) *Job Analysis: A manager's guide*. 2nd edn, London, IPD.

TORNOW, W. W. (1993) Perceptions or reality: is multi-perspective measurement a means or an end? *Human Resource Management*. Summer/Fall, Vol.32, Numbers 2–3, pp221–9.

6

DATA COLLECTION, REPORT FORMATS AND REPORT–PROCESSING

There's no accounting for taste.   Anon

The medium is the message.   Marshall McLuhan

Key points

☐ Data processing can be done in-house or by using an external bureau service.

☐ The choice of whether to go in-house rests on cost, resource and issues of perceived confidentiality.

☐ Methods of data collection can be paper questionnaires, disks or networks.

☐ Many different report formats are available in varying degrees of clarity and detail. They can be graphical, numerical, textual, or a combination of these.

☐ There are a number of ways in which reports can include summarised information.

☐ Report formats have different ways of assuring the respondent's anonymity.

Why do your own processing?

This chapter starts with a question similar to that which started Chapter 4. In other words, before we look at the various ways in which you can collect and process feedback data, let us first examine the pros and cons of doing it yourself as opposed to using an outside agency. These arguments revolve around issues of cost, resources, and confidentiality.

Cost

At the time of writing there are some 15 proprietary processing systems available on the British market. There are differences between them, and the checklist at the end of this chapter is intended to remove some of the confusion. Two of the biggest differences are in costs and method of payment. Most of the producers charge an up-front licence fee followed by a 'click' price. ('Clicks' or 'authorisations' represent one report each. The usual method of getting them is to obtain authorisations in advance.) Some sell an outright, unlimited usage licence. Some click prices are on a sliding scale depending on volume. The range of initial licence costs is from £1,000 to £80,000. Click prices vary from zero to £65 each. Potential users will be happy to know that the prices of most systems of this nature will go down rather than up! Other costs are sometimes made explicit, and sometimes not. These include an installation fee involving physical installation and training of administrators, and annual software support charges. Some licences are renewable annually. There are also various add-ons, for example self-development guides. There are also the one-off costs of purchasing dedicated computers and printers.

Many processing systems provide the capability to customise questionnaires and report formats. The main disadvantage is that they are relatively expensive. The cost of buying independence from the supplier of a proprietary questionnaire, or an external processing organisation, can appear to be high. As we have seen, outright purchase or leasing of proprietary systems can also be high. It is rarely justifiable for small-scale applications. The user must not forget to factor in other costs such as initial implementation and training support, on-going internal administration, and external technical support.

There are two main reasons for the high cost. The first is that with any new technology or development, initially prices are high but become lower as time goes by and the market increases. One has only to look at the computer industry to realise the extent to which this has happened. The second reason is the high initial investment that software suppliers need to make, particularly to build flexibility into the system. Giving the user the capability to do what they want to do, when and how they want to do it is a lengthy and expensive process. For example, the processing software used by one organisation took at least four highly qualified man years to design and take through numerous stages of development. Enhancements are also coming out at six-monthly intervals. Yet there is no system that will give total flexibility in questionnaire design and report formats. Even the best have limits.

Cheaper systems are available but with these come more limitations on customising capability, the number and type of questions, and alternative reporting formats.

The alternative to in-house processing is to use an outside bureau service. There are several of these, but fewer than there are system suppliers.They are usually dedicated, high volume operations using powerful hardware and flexible software packages. They charge per report produced, with prices ranging from about £40 to £150 depending on the type and numbers of reports. Most prices are in the £60–80 range. As with purchased systems, prices are likely to go down unless some new type of service is developed.

The prospective 360-degree feedback user basically needs to calculate what their annual usage and its frequency are likely to be. At some point it becomes financially worthwhile to bring the processing in-house by using a system of a given sophistication and cost. The less the system's flexibility, the lower the cost and therefore the lower the break even point. Some organisations would reach this level quite quickly; some would never reach it. Frequency is another issue because a steady flow of processing is probably easier to handle in-house than an avalanche of work once a year or less. Bureau service operators are better able to handle peaks and troughs.

Resources

The days of using calculators or spread sheets to process questionnaires are probably numbered. They are being replaced by a more high-tech era, based on more sophisticated software. Despite this, it is surprising to discover how much administrative and clerical work the process entails. Half the systems available are not networked, relying primarily on paper questionnaires. Thus forms have to be printed, distributed, collected, collated, and chased up. Data has to be hand-entered or scanned in. Reports have to be assembled. Quality has to be assured. The consequences of error can be serious.

Table 9 shows a quality control check-list used for such a system.

Networking removes the need for paper and that represents a saving in administrative cost. A sophisticated, heavy-duty, networked system will do a lot of work automatically and quickly. Yet someone still needs to define the project specification, create an instrument, define demographics, assign participants and respondents, and organise and monitor data collection. They have to select or customise report formats and set this up on the computer, then organise the printing of reports. Someone else may have to set up administrator modules, create administrator and user accounts, and handle errors.

Again, therefore, it is a matter of deciding what time and resources you are prepared to expend on carrying out these tasks in-house. You also need to replace anyone who leaves or is transferred with someone who is equally well trained.

Confidentiality

Whereas costs and resource are basically economic considerations, the issue of confidentiality and trust is fundamentally different. External processing enables the organisation to assure itself and its employees that very sensitive feedback data does not get into the wrong hands. Information can accidentally go astray, completed questionnaires can be sent back to the wrong person, unauthorised people can accidentally see reports which are confidential. In theory (although I personally have never encountered this) the organisation or its representatives could use the information for the wrong purposes, such as selection for redundancy or demotion.

When briefing participants the most commonly asked questions concern confidentiality in some way or other:

☐ What is behind all this?

☐ Why are they *really* doing this?

Table 9

AN EXAMPLE OF INTERNAL/EXTERNAL BUREAU SERVICE – CHECK-LIST

Open-ended answers
- ☐ Open-ended answers typed up and proof-read by the operator and one other person.
- ☐ Open-ended answers in correct format for that client.
- ☐ Participant's name appears on each page of open-ended answers.

Pre-scanning
- ☐ All sections of questionnaire have been filled in properly, ie in pencil, and without duplication or omissions.
- ☐ All codes have been checked by the operator and one other person.
- ☐ The order of the questionnaires is the same as on the tracking sheet.
- ☐ The number of participants and respondents in data file is the same as on the tracking sheet.
- ☐ The questions are descrambled correctly (where necessary).
- ☐ The processing notes are up to date before printing the report.
- ☐ Check against report requirements and the fax approved by the client for the report layout (if no approved fax, check with consultant and get approval).

Report
- ☐ The number of participants in batch (is the same as on the tracking sheet).
- ☐ The number of respondents in each report (is the same as on the tracking sheet).
- ☐ Check some of the self-report against the self-questionnaire.
- ☐ Check three of the questions on one report from each batch to make sure that the scores for one respondent group are correct (for example, peers).
- ☐ The participant's name is on each page of the report.
- ☐ Explanatory notes included when necessary.
- ☐ Open-ended answers included when necessary.
- ☐ Anything extra or different this time – for example, summaries or proformas, etc? (Check notes and correspondence.)
- ☐ Reports are in the correct client covers, if applicable.
- ☐ Check whom to send the report to, and what to send with it, eg copies of the report or tracking sheets.

☐ Who will see my report? My boss? Personnel? (and if so, who in Personnel?) My colleagues?

☐ My staff? The board?

□ Will it be used to consider me for promotion? If so, will potential bosses see it?

□ Will it be used for pay?

The same fears can arise when briefing respondents:

□ Who will read the questionnaire I complete?

□ How do you prevent my boss or colleague from knowing what I said?

□ What happens if the boss finds out?

If people do not feel reassured about confidentiality they may still take part in the feedback project, but how much can their feedback be relied upon in these circumstances?

Some organisations enjoy levels of trust among their employees that make people sure that whatever they say in confidence will be respected by their employer. The latter's systems are watertight, so that data leaks hardly ever occur. Employees' feelings about confidential matters and personal issues of sensitivity are taken very seriously. The employees understand this.

Other organisations have a much more open culture than others. Employees feel free to speak their minds on the issues without fear of recrimination. Nobody is penalised for saying what they think. People are not afraid of feedback. They are used to giving feedback to each other and know how to accept it. In circumstances such as these confidentiality and anonymity are just not issues, and the decision to process in-house can rest solely on costs and resources.

Methods of data collection

Data collection technology is more advanced in the USA than in Europe, so it might be as well to look firstly at the alternatives that are appearing, or that are already available over there. It is important for the potential user to consider the various data collection alternatives. The choice of method will depend on the existing in-house technology, the size of application, the sophistication of respondents, and the culture of the organisation.

Paper questionnaires

Questionnaires may be scannable or non-scannable. Some scannable questionnaires require an optical mark reader to 'read' marks made by the respondent on the rating scales. The great advantage of this technology is that it enables very fast reading and data entry into the processing system. Some scanners will read ink. Some will read pencil. Some can read only off special paper and special ink, and require highly accurate printing processes enabling marks on specific parts of the page to be accurately registered. All this makes for a specialised design and printing set-up that is beyond all but the most sophisticated in-house printing departments. In the United Kingdom there are two main suppliers of scannable questionnaires – NCSi and Data and Research Services – both of which provide a design and printing service.

The cost of scannable forms can be somewhat higher than that of a more simple desk-top published version, but they do have the considerable advantage of speed. The forms also look very professional, thus adding to the credibility of the questionnaire. Basically, they make possible the speedy and extremely accurate processing of large numbers of forms. (In contrast, the more laborious alternative of hand-entry does not possess this capability.) They are particularly useful if the same questionnaire has to be used for large numbers of people. However, frequent revision or alteration inevitably adds to the cost.

The alternative is to design and print your own questionnaires, and then hand-enter the data. Most desk-top publishing systems can now produce a professional looking finish, and in-house or external printing can add to it. Such forms are also less costly to alter. However, the user has to trade off the time and resources required to hand-enter data via a keyboard. It also needs far more attention to quality control because of potential inaccuracies in transcription.

A final word on paper questionnaires: a frequent objection by potential users is that those taking part in the project might disappear under a mountain of paper. After all 300 participants can generate 3,000 questionnaires between them and their respondents. Experience suggests that this fear rarely materialises. 360-degree feedback projects are spread across the organisation. Individuals themselves do not therefore encounter large numbers of questionnaires. In cases where individuals might have too many to complete themselves, the organising department can step in to limit the number of forms that one person receives. Overall then, this problem is rarely as severe in practice as people expect.

One final disadvantage of all paper questionnaires, whether scannable or not, is that technology has not yet found a fool-proof way of transcribing hand-written open-ended responses. These still, therefore, require the attention of a typist. Microsoft estimate that reliable handwriting recognition systems are three to five years away.

Disks

Some questionnaires are available on floppy disk. In this method of data collection the participant receives the questions on disk. The disk will be set up to receive data from a given number of respondents. The participant taps in their answers to the rated questions and also types in any open-ended responses. They then review their responses, lock their input, and send the disk to their first respondent. After they have completed the questionnaire this person sends the disk on to the next respondent. Issues of confidentiality are solved by installing a locking device that makes it impossible for anyone other than the administrator to access other people's answers.

Questionnaires are easy to read on screen as Figure 11 shows.

The advantage of this method is that the number of individual questionnaires being posted around the organisation goes down from perhaps ten per participant to one. The presentation of questions makes them easy to read. Minimal computer literacy is required, and the method might appeal to employees who already use a personal computer for many of their work activities. The one big drawback seems to be time. One disk circulating among up to ten respondents inevitably will take longer than ten pieces of paper circulating in parallel. It is difficult to identify, and therefore chase up, stragglers. One tardy, disorganised or absent respondent can slow up everyone else. Two can be a disaster. Of course, you can send more than one disk and collate the data at the end. Another big advantage is that no manual transcription of open-ended

Figure 11

ON-SCREEN QUESTIONNAIRE

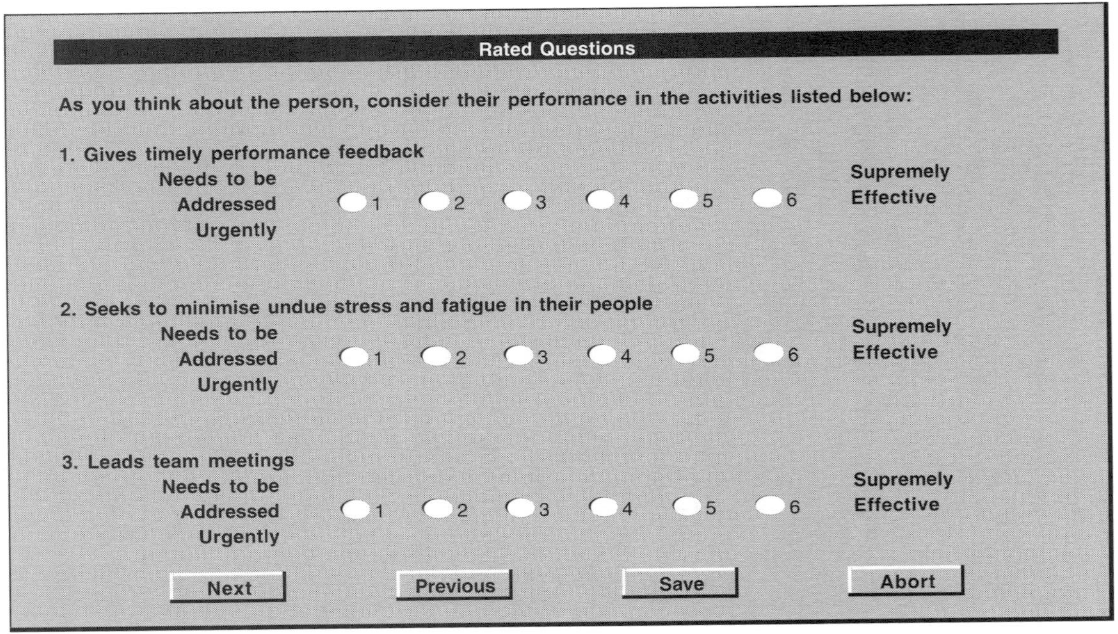

Rated Questions

As you think about the person, consider their performance in the activities listed below:

1. Gives timely performance feedback

Needs to be Addressed Urgently   1 2 3 4 5 6   Supremely Effective

2. Seeks to minimise undue stress and fatigue in their people

Needs to be Addressed Urgently   1 2 3 4 5 6   Supremely Effective

3. Leads team meetings

Needs to be Addressed Urgently   1 2 3 4 5 6   Supremely Effective

| Next | Previous | Save | Abort |

responses is involved, thus reducing the chance of in-accuracies creeping in.

Networks

Specialised software is now becoming available to enable 360-degree feedback projects to be run on networks. Typically, in these systems the respondent calls up the questionnaire on their terminal, and completes and sends it electronically. It is possible to track, collect, and process centrally all responses. Feedback reports can be provided as hard copy or on screen.

The main advantage of such systems is that they enable large-scale users to implement 360-degree feedback in all parts of the organisation with minimal fuss. Information can be collected quickly and easily. It can be stored and accessed. The user can readily manipulate the data to look not just at individuals but at demographic differences. They also present the large-scale user with the opportunity to link the system to their other human resources systems, thus providing additional information for performance appraisal, career counselling, succession planning, and performance-based pay.

Report formats

The key principle in choosing a reporting format for the results of your 360-degree feedback questionnaire is, as with many other decisions on this subject, a matter of clarity and detail. Too much detail will confuse or even antagonise the reader. Too much simplicity will again confuse because there may not be enough detail to work on in terms of knowing their strengths and development areas, and doing something about them.

For example, in Chapter 4 I said that in my opinion measuring behaviour at the competency level is usually not enough to give clear performance improvement pointers. This is reinforced if we look at how such results might be presented.

Let us look at a very simple and clear bar chart in Figure 12.

The participant can rightly deduce from this that their performance in taking responsibility and control is not seen as very strong. Unfortunately, no other conclusions are possible. Because there is no more detail available the participant does not know, for example, which elements of taking responsibility

Figure 12

COMPETENCY-LEVEL REPORT

Participant Name

Survey Name

Profile and Analysis Report

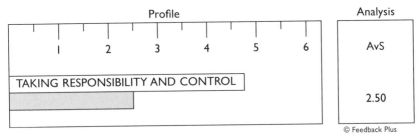

are causing the problem. Is it all of them or only specific ones? Indeed, what are the elements?

So let us take this format into a deeper level of detail by including the behavioural items shown in Figure 13.

We now know which elements within the competency are causing the problem. Whereas this person takes ownership of problems and faces up to conflict, they are less effective at delivering what they have promised, staying in control, or using other people. So, by examining performance at the item level we are giving some much more specific clues to the participant.

But are all the respondents saying this? We cannot tell from the presentation in Figure 13. So let us look at the specific respondent groups shown in Figure 14. Again we will go deeper into the detail.

We can now see that staff and peers rate this behaviour differently. Staff seem to be saying that in situations involving them they see little or no problem. Peers are saying the opposite. So perhaps the participant should be concentrating on situations or meetings involving peers?

One more level of detail might be to take the scores and show the range from highest to lowest. Perhaps we would even show the spread of scores. In Figure 15 the highest score for peers is 3 and the lowest is 1.

The point that Figure 15 makes is that the more detailed the format the greater the usefulness of the data. The more specific the feedback on individual items from different groups of people,

Figure 13

ITEM-LEVEL REPORT

Participant Name
Survey Name
Profile and Analysis Report

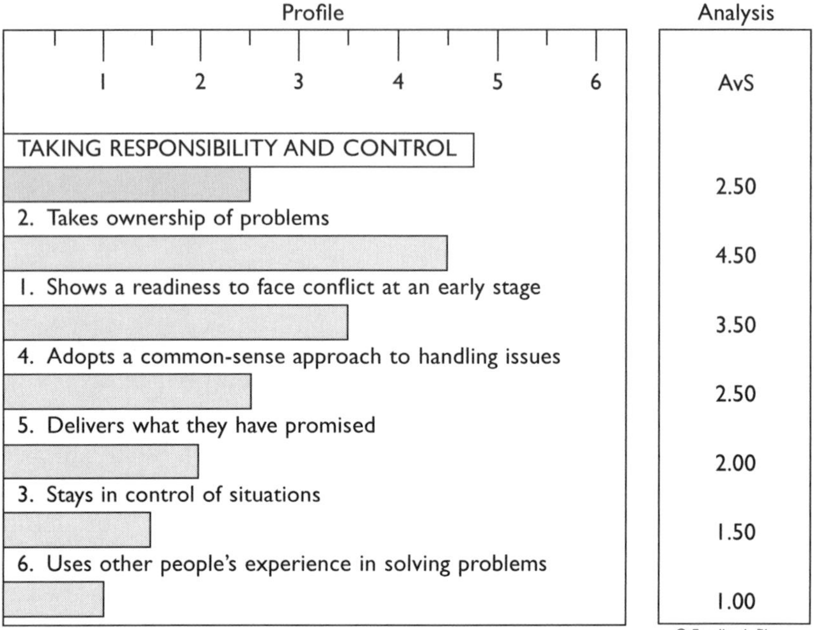

Profile	Analysis

1	2	3	4	5	6	AvS

TAKING RESPONSIBILITY AND CONTROL

2.50

2. Takes ownership of problems

4.50

1. Shows a readiness to face conflict at an early stage

3.50

4. Adopts a common-sense approach to handling issues

2.50

5. Delivers what they have promised

2.00

3. Stays in control of situations

1.50

6. Uses other people's experience in solving problems

1.00

© Feedback Plus

and the more information there is about the nature of the scores, the easier it is to understand what people are saying. The more detail with which we provide the participant the easier it is to take action to improve performance.

On the other hand, do you remember the illustration in Chapter 4 (page 84) in which we calculated what is involved in reading a 100 item questionnaire in a quite common format? Items themselves can be very specific and clear, but what about the impact made by a report of dozens of pages? Could it be counter-productive?

So the report format you choose needs to be a well thought out trade-off between detail and impact. Too little detail can mean useless generality. Too much can be confusing. You can achieve the happy medium only by considering the purpose of the instrument, and the sophistication of the participants.

Figure 14

RESPONDENT GROUPS' REPORT

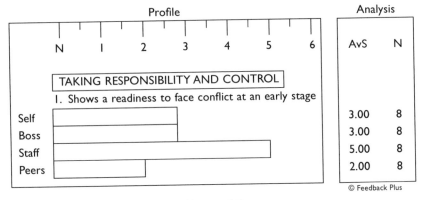

Participant Name
Survey Name
Perspectives Report

Figure 15

HIGHEST/LOWEST SCORES

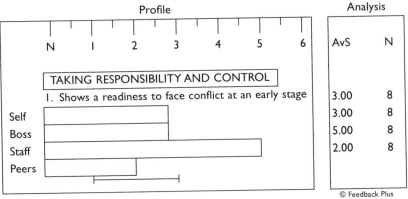

Participant Name
Survey Name
Perspectives Report

We are going to look at the three main ways in which feedback appears: graphically, numerically, and in text form. In practice, many good report formats actually combine all three, but for now it is best to look at them separately, because they all present different issues.

Graphical formats
Most of the choices appear as graphs, so this seems the most appropriate place to start.

We have already seen an example of how simple bar charts can give a clear, graphical presentation. As mentioned earlier, the most acceptable formats seem to be those which combine both clarity and detail – not always the easiest balance to achieve.

Figure 16 is another version that uses line graphs to achieve the same result.

In this example, information shows what each respondent group thinks of the participant's performance on each question. Other than the layout, the difference is that standardised scores have been used. Thus, additional information is available, ie how the individual's performance compares with that of a norm group.

One criticism of the use of norm groups is that they may not (or more importantly, may not *seem* to) be an appropriate comparison for the individual. In one of our lighter moments we have recorded the main ways (21 of them!) in which people seek to avoid feedback. Certainly, the answer 'The norm group is not representative of me, my job, or my level in the organisation' can be used as a get-out. On the other hand norming can indeed be useful to people to know where they stand in relation to others.

Another way to do this is to create company norms. For example Coopers and Lybrand, in one of their 360-degree feedback instruments, show how the participant compares to their peers, as can be seen in Figure 17.

All participants (about 200 of them) are from the same level in the organisation and, even though from different disciplines, share the same type of client. This section of their reports shows the individual's score from all respondents against each question as compared to the average score achieved by everyone who took part in the programme. In a competitive organisation participants welcome such data because the comparisons are seen as extremely valid and useful.

In Chapter 4 we looked at the use of dual scales as a more accurate means of showing people not just how well they perform, but how important a particular behaviour actually is.

Figure 16

LINE GRAPH REPORT

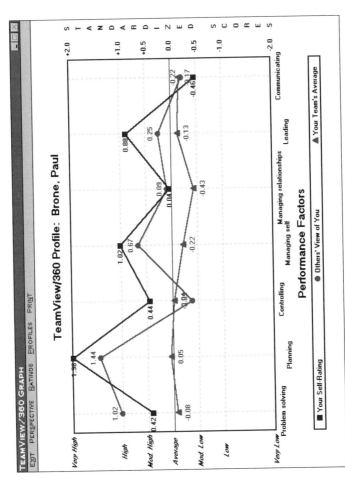

© Advanced Teamware

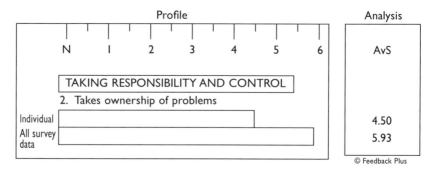

Figure 17

NORMS

Participant Name
Survey Name
Individual *v* Group Comparison Report

In Figure 18 the two scales (in this case Importance and Performance) are shown together for each respondent group. By comparing them the participant is able to see the gap – positive or negative – between the two levels, and therefore establish a list of priorities.

In Figure 19 we have a more sophisticated presentation of gap analysis. Notice that in this format the concentration is primarily on the size of the gap between C (current frequency of behaviour) and E (expected frequency of behaviour). Although the levels of C and E can be identified, the emphasis is on the gap itself. The greater the gap, wherever it happens to be on the scale, the greater the need for change. The smaller the gap, the more effective the performance because the closer it is to expectations. The Recommendation column automatically generates comments, such as four stars for a strong performer, two stars for a small gap and the word INCREASE where improvement is clearly required.

Some final words on graphical formats

The number of processing systems on the market is increasing as 360-degree feedback grows in popularity. The simplest systems will give just one non-customisable presentation. The most sophisticated systems will provide many alternatives. However, one mistake that prospective purchasers frequently make is to assume that the processing system is a glorified

Figure 18

IMPORTANCE v PERFORMANCE

Participant Name

Survey Name

Perspectives Report

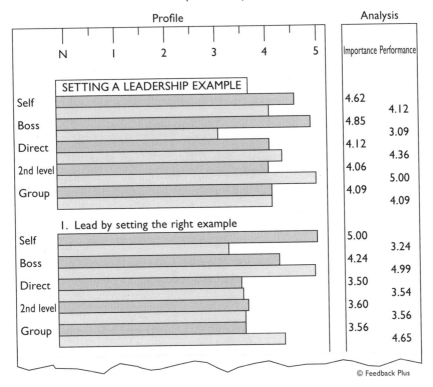

© Feedback Plus

Figure 19

CURRENT v EXPECTED

Analysis by behaviour

Behaviour	N	AGS	Average gap size C–E				Gaps					Recommendation
			1 2 3 4 5				0	1	2	3	4	
2. Express ideas clearly												
Self	1	1.00	C ■■■ E					1				* *
Boss A	1	1.00	C ■■■ E					1				* *
Staff/Support A	3	0.66	C ■■ E				2		1			* *
Peers A	2	1.50	C ■■■ E					1	1			Increase

© CCI Assessment and Development Group

desk-top publishing system that can produce any format required, or make the minutest changes to standard formats. Such changes are possible, but only at some expense because of the need to reprogramme the software, and re-test it.

Most suppliers produce standard formats based on their own research and experience, and that of their clients. The more forward looking ones constantly enhance their products, bringing out new formats or variations. However, to commission individual, tailor-made alterations can be an expensive business. Sometimes the expense is out of all proportion to the scale of changes required, and can make little or no difference to the impact of the feedback data. You need to be very careful about going down this route.

The best advice, at least to a client who is new to 360-degree feedback, is to experiment with different standard systems or formats before going down the route of customisation. Unfortunately, the choice of feedback format can be about as objective as choosing wallpaper – hence the quotation at the beginning of this chapter! The strongly held views of the person making the decision may be quite different from those of the feedback recipient. The answer lies in research, experimentation, piloting and acting on feedback.

Numerical formats
Numerical formats were a predecessor of their graphical equivalents. Many can be produced from graphics packages like Excel, or as part of the new computerised systems.

To my mind, formats like the one in Figure 20 that rely purely on a numerical presentation are less effective than combined formats. There are two reasons for this. Labouring over lists of figures can be tedious and time consuming. It is often more difficult to draw lessons out of such a presentation. The second reason is that business is becoming ever more presentation-conscious. Managers are used to attending presentations or reading reports where complex information is presented in a compelling visual way. It is not uncommon, for example, to attend a major conference where the speakers have produced their presentations on PowerPoint with very good illustrations and coloured graphics. Contrast this with the speaker who comes along with some figures typed onto an overhead transparency. No contest!

Figure 20

SPREADSHEET–PRODUCED REPORT

Question Questions in each section are displayed in order of effectiveness	Level of Effectiveness						Need to Demonstrate					
	Self	Boss	Peers	Staff	Clients	Average	Self	Boss	Peers	Staff	Clients	Average
Planning and Organising												
7 Completes work within an agreed time frame	4.0	4.0	5.0	4.3	4.0	4.4	4.0	4.0	5.0	4.1	3.0	4.3
18 Achieved goals through realistic planning	4.0	4.0	5.0	3.7	4.0	4.0	3.0	4.0	4.0	4.0	4.0	4.0
12 Sets clear objectives	5.0	4.0	4.0	4.0	3.0	3.9	4.0	4.0	4.5	4.3	5.0	4.4
4 Uses their time effectively	3.0	4.0		3.7		3.8	3.0	4.0	2.0	4.0		3.6
8 Checks to ensure plans are on course	4.0	3.0	3.0	4.3	3.0	3.6	4.0	4.0	3.5	4.3	3.0	3.9

In modern business presentations the medium and style are all important. There are many messages competing with 360-degree feedback for the individual's attention, and only the best presented will get a hearing or be remembered.

Textual formats

We have seen in Chapter 4 that open-ended questions can add a great deal to the power of the questionnaire. They allow people to break free from the structured, rated questions and express their views in their own words. You might think that the presentation of the answers is a simple transposition job for the typist to do. In fact there are some important principles of best practice which we recommend people to observe.

Table 10 presents two lists of open-ended answers. The answers are the same, but the presentation is different:

Table 10

OPEN-ENDED ANSWERS

Comments made by respondents
What do you see as this person's key strength?
My friend Meg is a good thinker.
I am very good at delegating.
Margaret is very good at time management.
Margaret has very high technical knowledge.
She always gets the job done on time.
Maggie is an ace at controlling others.
Main strength is the ability to relate to people.
Mrs Wells is a very kind person to me.
She has a good brain.
Margaret has extremly well-developed analytical skills.

Please describe the main area where this person should change in order to improve their performance?
When Maggie gives me things to do, she doesn't explain matters very well.
A tendency to overcontrol her staff.
I sometimes wish Margaret would explain things so that we lesser mortals could understand them.
Margaret tends to take on to much work herself.
Her continual demonstration of intellectual superiority really annoys me; she ought to help people more.
Mrs Wells has no weaknesses that I would like to comment on.
Doesn't give me interesting things to do.
Margaret tends to overpower her team members, including me.
I am too much of a perfectionist at times.
Meg's a good chap, but she does tend to dominate people. A bit too bosy.

Comments made by respondents

What do you see as this person's key strength?
Self
I am very good at delegating.
Boss
Main strength is the ability to relate to people.
Staff
She always gets the job done on time.
Margaret is very good at time management.
Maggie is an ace at controlling others.
Mrs Wells is a very kind person to me.
Peers
Margaret has very high technical knowledge.
Margaret has extremly well developed analytical skills.
My friend Meg is a good thinker.
She has a good brain.

Please describe the main area where this person should change in order to improve their performance?
Self
I am too much of a perfectionist at times.
Boss
A tendency to overcontrol her staff.
Staff
Doesn't give me interesting things to do.
Margaret tends to take on to much work herself.
When Maggie gives me things to do, she doesn't explain matters very well.
Mrs Wells has no weaknesses that I would like to comment on.
Peers
I sometimes wish Margaret would explain things so that we lesser mortals could
   understand them.
Margaret tends to overpower her team members, including me.
Meg's a good chap, but she does tend to dominate people. A bit too bosy.
Her continual demonstration of intellectual superiority really annoys me; she
   ought to help people more.

Either presentation is acceptable. The second one, in which the answers are classified by respondent group, is more helpful. Yet it also makes the identification of respondents easier, by showing which group they belong to.

You will also notice in this particular example that there are some spelling errors and marked stylistic differences between respondents. Some organisations would give in to the temptation to 'tidy them up'. I would advise against it. Any correction is a move away from what the respondent has actually said, and may be a wrong interpretation. Ungrammatical feedback, if provided, is what the participant should read because that is *exactly* what the respondent wrote.

The same applies to unreadable words, if the feedback is provided in handwriting. If the writing is illegible, guessing can be dangerous and may result in a word the respondent did not actually write. Again, this is an unintentional misinterpretation of the original, and it should be avoided. A better practice in these instances is to insert question marks.

Remember, the purpose in recording open-ended answers is not to provide a sanitised, grammatically pure edition of what the respondent has written. It is to record, not interpret.

Summaries

Some software systems automatically produce summarised information which can help the reader to identify the key parts of the feedback. Here are two examples. The summary in Table 11 shows the highest and lowest rated behaviours of the participant.

The summary in Table 12 calculates the frequency with which a behaviour is identified by respondent groups as a development need. A window around the item number shows that at least two groups identified it. No windows show that it was identified by only one group.

It is important to distinguish between a summary and a commentary. The former is a replay of the information in shortened form. The latter leans more towards interpretation, because information has been selected as significant and commented on. Commentaries are a method of facilitation, which is covered in the next chapter.

A final point on report formats: it is essential to think through how the report should be structured. What order should the sections be in? Should there be an introduction or summary?

Explanatory sheets

Although face-to-face facilitation will help the participant to

Table 11

SUMMARISED INFORMATION

TeamView/360™
Advanced Teamware Publishing, Inc

Team: SAMPLE
Subject: Jones, Jeff
Title: TeamView/360™ Top and Bottom Five Individual Behaviours
Date: 13/05/97

These behaviours were identified by your co-workers on the IBQ as your greatest strengths. They are rank ordered so the first item is your most effective behaviour. These are the areas in which you contribute most to the success of the team:

Score	Behaviour
1.05	Developing oneself
1.02	Adapting to change
0.88	Handling pressure
0.85	Articulating ideas
0.79	Coping with own frustration

The following five behaviours were identified by your co-workers on the IBQ as those in which your performance is least effective. They are rank ordered so the first item is the behaviour that received the lowest score. We suggest you pay particular attention to these five and focus your immediate developmental activities on them:

Score	Behaviour
−0.47	Resolving conflicts
−0.17	Monitoring performance
−0.09	Listening
−0.06	Giving recognition
0.04	Responding to feedback

understand their feedback, the report should also contain an explanation of how to read the graphs. An example is shown in Table 13.

Table 12

SUMMARY OF DEVELOPMENT NEEDS

Leadership Assessment Survey   Date:

Participant Name:

Company Name:

Developmental needs (by frequency)

Diversity (4)

	5	Make the effort to work co-operatively with others
	9	Negotiate differences of opinion openly and fairly
	12	Accept differences of opinion
	23	Demonstrate a willingness to be flexible and 'open minded'
	31	Express his/her point of view in a tactical way
	49	Bring together people with varied talents and perspectives to resolve work group problems

Empowerment (3)

	10	Give you/others visibility on key projects, tasks
	61	Promote co-operation and collaboration within the work group
	74	Allow you/others to initiate actions
	77	Involve you/others in up-front planning on key projects
	92	Provide critical information for you/others to do your job

Motivating (3)

	16	Provide you/others with a sense of belonging to the work group
	40	Praise you for a specific job well done

Planning and goal setting (3)

	33	Develop realistic plans for reaching goals
	59	Use his/her time effectively
	73	Provide you/others with realistic time lines for projects

Teamwork (3)

	7	Share credit and recognition for accomplishments with others
	18	Explain how each person's performance impacts on the work of others
	25	Capitalise on your personal strengths when leading group projects
	47	Co-ordinate work priorities with you/others
	84	Work across functional groups to achieve company goals

Initiative and risk taking (2)

	8	Take prompt action when unexpected opportunities arise
	38	Persevere despite organisational obstacles

© CCI Assessment and Development Group

Anonymity

In most 360-degree feedback systems anonymity is guaranteed to respondents. Feedback report formats try to honour this

Table 13

SAMPLE OF EXPLANATION TEXT

Understanding your 360-degree feedback report

Explanation of profile and analysis report

This report shows you how often people are aware of you performing certain behaviours at the moment. It presents the grouped responses as a set of bars on the left of the page, and in numerical format on the right.

The bar length corresponds with the Average Score (AvS) for each question, which is shown in the first numerical column. A high number means that, on average, you were rated highly for that question, ie that behaviour is seen often. A low number indicates that a behaviour is not seen often.

The second column (N) shows the number of raters who answered the question.

The final column (AgS) shows the degree to which people agreed about your performance. A number close to 0 means that people could not agree about how often they see a certain behaviour. A number close to 1 shows a consensus of opinions about your current performance.

promise in several ways. First it is usual only for the boss to be identified individually. In this sense the boss is fair game, because it is part of their job to give feedback anyway. But for other respondents the view is that the cloak of anonymity will encourage them to be more forthright than they would be on a face-to-face basis with the participant. This is something of an over-generalisation. I have encountered situations in which the participant shares their feedback with others, only for respondents not only to reveal quite freely what they said, but also to expand on it. However, it is reasonable to suppose that many people will feel happier about giving honest feedback if they know they will not be identified with it.

Anonymity can be achieved in several ways. The first is to make sure that completed questionnaires do not come back to the recipient but are collected by some secure source inside or outside the organisation. When it comes to processing the report the scores of individual members of respondent groups are usually averaged. However, for those participants tempted to try to find out who said what there are a number of safe-guards available.

If the number in the group is small, for example two or three, then this can encourage speculation. Only one of them has to omit a question and the number becomes even more vulnerable. Many systems have their own ways of dealing with such situations. Most have a cut-off figure below which a particular questionnaire score will not appear.

However, the only effective way to guarantee anonymity for individuals is to apply the 'safety in numbers' theory seriously. This means making sure that respondent group sizes are big enough, with, say, four or more people in them. It may mean starting with a larger number to allow for dropouts. It can also entail a determined and organised attempt at chasing up late returns.

Check-list for deciding whether to process in-house or externally

☐ Do the projected usage and frequency justify in-house processing over a bureau service?

☐ What extra resources will I need for administration, technical support etc?

☐ What are the actual and apparent implications for confidentiality of going in-house?

Check-list for selecting a bureau service

☐ What report formats are available?

☐ What data collection methods can be accommodated?

☐ What is the turnaround time?

☐ Do they do emergency processing?

☐ What methods of delivery are required to and from the processing centre?

☐ What is the price?

☐ What exactly do I get for the money?

☐ What are their quality control procedures?

☐ What is their track record on reliability?

Check-list for selecting an in-house processing system

Data collection
What means of data collection is/are employed?

- ☐ Scannable forms or hand entry from paper questionnaires?
- ☐ Disk-based?
- ☐ Networkable?

Questionnaire customisation
- ☐ Are a pre-set competency framework and questions already built into the software?
- ☐ How easily can they be changed?
- ☐ If questionnaires can be customised what are the limits to the number of competencies and items?
- ☐ If there is an item bank of pre-written questions available, how were they developed and validated?
- ☐ What are the choices on scales available?
- ☐ What are the limitations on number, type and titles of respondents?

Report formats
- ☐ What main types of format are available?
- ☐ What capacity is there for further customisation?
- ☐ Is colour printing available?
- ☐ Can reports be shown on screen as well as in hard copy?
- ☐ Can reports (and questionnaires) be printed in foreign languages?
- ☐ Do reports contain ready-made development suggestions, and if so to what level of detail?

Processing and administration
- ☐ What internal resources are required to administer questionnaires, and for tracking, report processing and printing?
- ☐ How user-friendly is the software to operate?
- ☐ What provisions exist within the software to safeguard anonymity and confidentiality?
- ☐ Can these be overridden?

Support

- [ ] What experience does the supplier have of 360-degree feedback in general?
- [ ] What training is given for installation?
- [ ] What subsequent technical support is available?
- [ ] Does the supplier operate their own bureau service?
- [ ] What is the supplier's policy on enhancements?
- [ ] What is their policy on re-programming?
- [ ] Is the supplier qualified to advise on best practice?
- [ ] Can the supplier provide training in facilitation?

Purpose

- [ ] Is the system a stand-alone 360-degree feedback system or does it include other HR systems, eg competency modelling?
- [ ] Can it link in with my own HR systems?

Price

- [ ] Does the price match the purpose and usage I have in mind?
- [ ] Is there a licence fee?
- [ ] Is this one-off or renewable?
- [ ] Is there a click price?
- [ ] What is the installation fee?
- [ ] Is there a training fee?
- [ ] Is consultancy support provided?
- [ ] Is there a maintenance fee?
- [ ] What optional extras are available and what is their cost?
- [ ] Are there any guarantees or warranties?

Other questions

- [ ] How was the software tested?
- [ ] Who is currently using it?

7

FACILITATION AND ACTION-PLANNING

There is not one whom we employ who does not, like ourselves, desire recognition, praise, gentleness, forbearance, patience.

Henry Word Beecher

People are usually convinced by reasons they discovered them-selves than by those found by others. Blaise Pascal

Key points

- [ ] The term facilitator means 'someone who makes things easier'.
- [ ] Facilitation of 360-degree feedback presents different challenges to the facilitator.
- [ ] Key facilitator competencies are vision, dealing with others, critical thinking and communication.
- [ ] Facilitating feedback involves planning and preparation as well as interpersonal skills.
- [ ] There are various ways, such as providing commentaries, of augmenting the facilitation session.
- [ ] Action planning, including development planning, re-quires attention not only to detail but also to prioritisation.

What is facilitation?

According to Collins Dictionary, 'to facilitate' means 'to make easier', or 'to assist the progress of'. It is a term that has become much used in recent years, particularly in the human resources and consultancy fields. Facilitation is required in many situations in which people are interacting with each other. This includes those in which feedback is being given and received. In a team-building situation the facilitator is called in to use specific techniques to help the team to understand how it is working and to improve its effectiveness as a group. The facilitator's role is to concentrate on team and interactive processes and help the team learn as a unit. A slight variation of this is sometimes called 'meetings facilitation'. At these events, those present do not necessarily constitute a team. They are often a collection of individuals, who may not normally work together, but are present for a specific purpose or project. In these situations the facilitator can adopt a team-building role, but is more often likely to concentrate on the analysis or data handling processes the team uses. These are not quite the same as interactive or interpersonal skills. They are more to do with methods of dealing with information: to set priorities, to develop creative ideas, to assess risks, and to look for the causes of problems.

In the psychometric field, people receive feedback on assessments they have completed, be these personality inventories or aptitude tests. Test producers have laid great emphasis on rigorous training and accreditation of test users. This helps to ensure that participants receive their feedback in a clear, sensitive manner. The type of facilitation called for in these circumstances is often a counselling or coaching approach, in addition to mere explanation of the results.

But 360-degree feedback is a newer phenomenon, presenting different challenges to the facilitator. The key difference is that facilitators can find themselves in many types of feedback situation, rather than being able to specialise. The full range of facilitation skills has to be deployed, making great demands on the individual. First, the feedback can be both detailed and extensive. The skills required to help someone cope with this are similar to the data-handling techniques involved in facilitating meetings. Drawing lessons from a mass of detail, deciding what to deal with first, and producing concrete action plans, may be the order of the day.

Second, the feedback can be surprising and possibly unpleasant at first sight. It can produce a variety of strong emotions which the facilitator must help the participant to deal with. Thus clarity of explanation, together with sensitivity of approach are required.

Third, the feedback does not necessarily remain solely in the hands of one individual. Facilitators can therefore find themselves enabling feedback-sharing with the boss or with other respondent groups. They can be asked to facilitate team feedback sessions. This may therefore call for the use of interactive team-building skills to help people get the best out of the event.

The skills model shown in Table 14 was originally developed for a group facilitators' training programme run by myself and my colleagues. It was intended to encompass the main behaviours which the facilitator needs constantly to demonstrate. The skills required for 360-degree feedback facilitation are substantially the same. Thus, behaviours around 'vision', such as keeping in mind the purpose of the meeting and recognising sensitive situations, are as relevant to individual situations as they are to groups. The same applies to other aspects of the model: 'dealing with others', by being able to resolve conflict and keep an open mind; 'critical thinking', discriminating between cause and effect and identifying key issues; 'communication', listening and reacting. We therefore have a behavioural specification, not only for group facilitators, but for a 360-degree feedback facilitator as well.

These behaviours are crucial to the facilitator's – and therefore the participant's – success. They are also very demanding.

Another model which some may find useful is the much simpler 'PCPC' approach, as shown in Figure 21 (page 145).

In this model both the facilitator and the participant between them carry out a balance of all four activities. The facilitator has a choice of which style to adopt. Thus, in some situations it is better if the facilitator does most of the 'presenting' by taking the participant through the report. In other situations it might be the participant who takes the facilitator through it. Similar choices appear in the other three aspects, ie the facilitator clarifies or gets the participant to do this by asking questions. The facilitator adopts a persuasive style to convince the reluctant participant that there might be some truth in the unpleasant news, or gets the participant to persuade him- or herself. Coaching is again a matter of style, with some

Table 14

FACILITATION SKILLS MODEL

Facilitation skills	
Vision	**Dealing with others**
☐ Clarifying the underlying purpose/objectives of meetings ☐ Contributing outside their own speciality ☐ Keeping the meeting on track ☐ Identifying group dynamics ☐ Recognising the different moods of a group ☐ Recognising sensitive situations ☐ Understanding roles	☐ Providing information to others willingly ☐ Reaching consensus ☐ Ensuring involvement of all participants ☐ Achieving win-win solutions ☐ Giving constructive feedback ☐ Being approachable and easy to talk with ☐ Being able to change their mind ☐ Entering the discussion with an open mind ☐ Handling sensitive situations
Communication	**Critical thinking**
☐ Expressing ideas clearly ☐ Listening without interrupting ☐ Intervening appropriately ☐ Asking open questions ☐ Listening actively ☐ Answering questions specifically ☐ Showing detachment	☐ Thinking logically ☐ Showing understanding of others' arguments ☐ Differentiating between cause and symptoms ☐ Exploring the underlying purpose of a decision ☐ Identifying the key issues quickly from a mass of detail ☐ Understanding complex arguments ☐ Thinking creatively ☐ Using appropriate facilitation tools

© Ward Dutton Partnership

facilitators adopting a more direct approach and others using the traditional questioning approach to achieve understanding and learning.

The job of the 360-degree feedback facilitator is to assist the participant to find their way through two of the most important stages of the feedback loop described in Chapter 1.

Figure 21

PRESENT, CLARIFY, PERSUADE, COACH

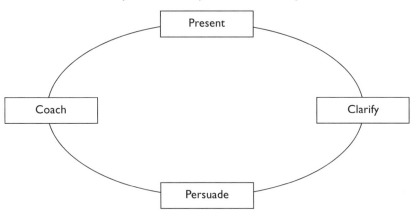

These are reflection and action planning. Reflection means understanding and internalising what the feedback says. Action planning means converting this understanding into a written statement of intent which describes what the participant will do differently and how they will achieve this.

Facilitating feedback for individuals

In this section I have included a list of the main lessons the facilitator should bear in mind when conducting a one-to-one feedback session. I use the word 'lessons' deliberately. They represent the main points that my colleagues and I have learned from hundreds of such sessions with a great variety of participants.

Preparation

Before any feedback session you should read the participant's report. Identify items of significance for you. These can be questions where there is unanimity that the participant is particularly effective or ineffective. They can also be questions where one or more groups are giving scores above or below other raters. Look for patterns of high or low scores. For example, is there some conceptual similarity between highest rated scores, or between the lowest rated questions? Does one respondent group rate consistently higher or lower than the others? How accurate is the self-perception?

You will also inevitably find areas that puzzle you. There may be inconsistencies, or some questions not answered by particular groups. Do not be surprised or alarmed if there are things you cannot explain. It is not your job to explain them. It *is* your job to work with the participant to achieve a full understanding of what is in the report. With some questions you may both start from a position where questions are raised rather than answered by the feedback report. This is one of the major ways in which 360-degree feedback differs from personality assessment feedback.

You are not, as a facilitator, in the position of interpreter. Preparation for a 360-degree feedback session is *not* all about you completely understanding the report and then explaining it all to the participant. Even if it was possible to understand everything, imagine the effect on the participant on hearing:

'You are very strong at listening, but your presentation skills are poor according to your peers. Your boss thinks your critical thinking is too imprecise. However, she likes the determination you display in difficult situations. Your action plan should be ... '. Perhaps there is a little too much emphasis on the 'Present' part of the feedback model!

I suspect that many participants and new facilitators approach 360-degree feedback thinking that it will be just as easy as that. It isn't! Graphs, numbers and text can have a deceptively precise and scientific aura. In reality, 360-degree feedback is the collection and presentation of necessarily subjective opinions about your performance. As we have seen in Chapter 1, what people actually perceive is real for them. However, the feedback sometimes asks more questions than it answers, and requires really hard work on the part of both participant and facilitator fully to understand the real meaning and implications.

Purpose of feedback

Although the participant may have been fully briefed in advance, this may have happened some time ago. They may have forgotten the main purpose of the feedback project. This may be the first occasion for some time that they have had the chance to talk to someone about it. This represents a good opportunity, therefore, to reassure them about any points of confidentiality, and to reiterate what the ground rules of the project are. These might cover:

- who is to see the information
- how this will happen. For example will the report go automatically to the boss? Will the participant have a choice of what data they reveal?
- arrangements or suggestions for sharing information with others.
- the rules to be observed on respecting anonymity of respondents. For example, I once sat in on a session where the participant was sharing and clarifying his feedback data with his direct reports. The contents of the report were on flipcharts and were then presented to the group. The style in which this was done (and I never knew whether it was deliberate or purely accidental) gave the distinct impression that the participant knew exactly what each respondent had said on each question. Whatever the motives behind this you can appreciate that respondents soon started to feel uncomfortable, and the session produced more mutual suspicion than open communication.

Roles
Explain who you are (the participant may never have met you before) and what your role is. The following points of explanation usually help the participant tune into you and your role:

- your position in the organisation (or outside it)
- any experience you have had of being on the receiving end!
- how you came to be in the position of facilitator (selection, training etc)
- how you intend to carry out your role, ie help the participant to understand their feedback and begin planning improvement action.

Explain the purpose of the session
This may be obvious to you, but may be far from obvious to the participant. The latter may have only the vaguest idea of what

to expect, or may have quite unrealistic expectations. As expectations are everything in situations like this, it is a good idea to agree a target outcome with the participant. Here are some targets in ascending order of ambitiousness (all are entirely valid, but are almost impossible to achieve in one session):

☐ to hand over the report
☐ to explain what the graphs and numbers represent
☐ to help the participant identify significant areas, eg uniformly high or low scores, or discrepancies between scores from different groups
☐ to help the participant understand what these mean
☐ to help the participant plan how they will clarify some of the questions raised
☐ to help the participant prioritise some of the areas for improvement
☐ to help the participant think of ways in which they will improve their performance
☐ to help the participant communicate to others how they will change and what changes to look for.

Agree a timescale

It should now be obvious that all the actions listed above cannot be covered in one session, however enlightened the participant and skilful the facilitator. In fact, 360-degree feedback is so powerful and contains so many surprises that it is expecting a lot of the participant to take everything on board at once.

A more useful strategy is to agree a timescale and a realistic minimum point to be reached. Thus, you might say something like:

'Let's agree that this session is going to last for 90 minutes. As a minimum in that time let us try to aim for a full understanding of what the graphical and numerical data really represent to you. If we manage that in time, let's spend the rest in setting some priorities for clarification or action. If we don't get very far with this, then we'll agree a time for another session.'

Notice also that there is very little mention of 'I' or 'you'. The implication is that you and the participant are a team that will work jointly on understanding the report; not the 'I' doing the telling, or the 'you' doing the listening.

Introductory comments

There are many ways of opening discussions like these. Most experienced facilitators develop their own ways of setting the participant at ease, and starting the feedback process. Here are a few that are often used:

- □ ask the participant what they thought of the process, their choice of respondents, or how it was communicated
- □ ask if they have had experience of feedback from other psychometric instruments, and, if so, what it was
- □ remind them of the questionnaire (show a copy if necessary)
- □ ask them what they expect their results to look like
- □ ask them how good at self-insight they think they are
- □ ask them to say what was in their last performance appraisal.

All of these are ways, not just of breaking the ice, but also of getting the participant to start focusing on the process and on themselves.

Whose responsibility is it anyway?

As we have said several times, 360-degree feedback puts the onus for action fairly and squarely on the shoulders of the participant. This starts at the feedback session. The data is theirs. The report is only about them. Your role is to help them understand the feedback and develop their own agenda for change. Your role is *not* to justify the report, or identify with it in anyway. If you find yourself slipping into a justification, stop. That is not why you are there.

Overheard during a facilitator training role play:

Facilitator: 'Well Jack, there seems to be a pattern emerging in many parts of your report. As you can see in these questions on communicating, your staff's scores are consistently lower than those of yourself or your boss.'

Participant: 'Too true. Why?'

Facilitator: 'I think the low scores are because they don't feel listened to, or talked with.'

Participant: 'I am really unhappy that my staff should have given me such low scores. What are you in Personnel going to do about them?'

Facilitator: 'Er ...'

In this example the participant managed to place responsibility on to his staff and on to 'Personnel', in fact everywhere but where it belonged.

Giving advice

Giving advice comes into the 'coaching' part of our PCPC model. Advice comes in many forms. It can mean explaining parts of the report, identifying patterns, or helping to plan action. However, the best advice is that which comes from within. Try, therefore, not to adopt the position of providing all the answers. Do not try to tell the person what to do. It is better to use questions to draw out from them what they should do.

A good way to clarify a problem situation is to ask the participant: 'Can you think of an example of what you do which causes this problem with this respondent group?' Often they can delve into their own experience to find examples.

It is sometimes useful to get the participant to think of why people have responded in the way they have, especially when the feedback data is surprising or unpalatable. It is another form of using examples. In other words, get them to answer the question: 'What specific things do I say or do that lead people to respond like this?' Somewhere in the answer there may be a clue to corrective action.

However, as we shall see later in this chapter, beware the answer: 'I can explain this.' It can be the start of a rationalisation designed to avoid the issue rather than resolve it.

Another way to use examples is to give your own. If you are an experienced manager or facilitator you should be able to think of occasions when you or others have encountered a similar problem to the one under discussion. Describing what you did, or what others did, is not telling the participant what to do. It is merely contributing a mini-case study and inviting them to learn from it.

Avoid generalities

To be useful, any plan for improved performance needs to be specific. This opportunity is provided by 360-degree feedback because of the details of performance which it reveals. Indeed, the very nature of the questions, when properly expressed in behavioural form, help clarify to the participant what they should do better, differently, more, or less. However, participants who are unused to this still seem to have difficulty in translating it into action. They assume that some magic next step is required. In practice, it is often much easier than that. For example, if someone does not score highly on an issue like 'telling people how their performance will be measured' it is relatively easy to break this down into sub-behaviours, such as:

□ decide on the type of performance measures you want for given tasks, for example quality, time, process etc

□ work out with the individual specifically what the quality measures are, or what will constitute quality performance

□ check that the individual understands these measures.

This is an important plan. It is simple, modest even. But it is specific.

This is far better than the participant leaving the meeting with the vague intention of 'improving my delegation skills'.

Another example: 'Improve my listening skills' is far better expressed as something like: 'In the next conversation I have with Angela I will reflect back to her at least two of her statements, in order to check my understanding.'

To make the feedback process worth the time and trouble there needs to be some demonstrable change in the person's behaviour. You therefore need to prevent the facilitation session deteriorating into 'good intentions'. The main questions to ask (and keep asking) are:

□ 'What can or will you do about it?'

□ 'How will you put this into practice?'

□ 'What will people see you doing or hear you saying when you have improved?'

Focus on priorities, or the 'domino effect'

Some 360-degree feedback is presented in great detail. It is usually of intense personal interest to the participant. However, I suggest that most people engaging in a personal improvement programme can cope with only a limited number of items in their action plan. Let us say about six, and no more than ten. The facilitator needs to help the participant to home in on the key activities that will make a difference. These will usually be the ones rated of high importance, and where performance is low when compared to expectations, or the norm group if one is used.

Often taking action on one development need will automatically result in an improvement in another. For example, if someone takes action to improve a behaviour such as 'letting people know what is expected of them' this will also help to improve performance in other areas such as objective-setting, delegation, measuring performance, or motivation. We call this the 'Domino Theory' which states that improvements in one area can have a knock-on effect on other areas. Therefore it is not only inadvisable to have very long lists of improvement actions: it should be unnecessary.

Seeking clarification

Despite the very specific nature of 360-degree feedback, it is sometimes necessary for the participant to seek clarification of what respondent groups are saying. This is quite in order, provided the rules of anonymity for respondents are not broken. For example, the boss's feedback is often identified individually. There should be no problem if the participant then wishes to obtain further information from him or her.

Dealing with other groups, however, should be approached with more care and it is the responsibility of the facilitator to advise the participant on how this might be done. You should, therefore, talk to the participant about how they will approach people and what they will say. It is usually not a good idea to approach individuals – unless the participant has convinced you that they have a particularly open and trusting relationship with the particular respondent. A better approach is to identify the next occasion on which the participant is likely to be meeting these people (whether subordinates or peers) as a group. Then discuss the best way of using the meeting to gain clarification. Participants might need coaching to draw the proper line between embarrassing respondents and approaching the issue too obliquely. If in doubt about the participant's ability to do this, then the facilitator should not recommend it.

A suggested routine for feedback sharing is given in Table 15.

It is very much part of your role as a facilitator to help the participant plan what they will say and how they will create a relaxed atmosphere at these sessions. It is an excellent idea to be present if possible. This will help both sides explore the issues fruitfully. In my experience, the most useful advice to give a participant in a feedback sharing session is to prepare them for the two 'moments of truth'. The first one of these is after the feedback has been presented and the participant asks 'Can anyone give me an example of what I do or say which causes this problem?' If this question is followed by silence then some gentle coaxing is required. If this fails, nothing further can be gained and you should not try. The second moment of truth is when the first unfavourable comment is made. If the participant rejects this, shows annoyance, or side-steps it, then nothing useful will follow. If, on the other hand, the participant responds positively then you are all probably in for a fruitful meeting.

Feedback sharing is not a high risk for some participants. There is evidence (described in more detail in Chapter 8) that indicates that feedback is more likely to be acted upon if it is shared, and that this should be encouraged rather than avoided.

Handling conflict

Inevitably, some of the news in a feedback report will be unwelcome. A colleague of mine sometimes refers to it as a cold shower. Later in this chapter there is a list of the most common ways people have of avoiding feedback like this. The list of avoidance techniques grows daily!

The facilitator's job is to help people face the music, not run away from it. Here are some tips on how to handle difficult situations.

- ☐ Balance bad news with good.
- ☐ Look at what the person *does* rather than talk about 'bad points'.
- ☐ If they wish to rationalise, let them get it out of their system. Then explain that, good or bad, accurate or inaccurate, justified or not, this is what people actually see. Is this a situation that the participant is prepared to tolerate?

Table 15

FIVE-STEP PROCESS

Use with your ☐ *Boss* ☐ *Others*	It is natural and normal for some discrepancies to occur when comparing your perception of a behaviour with the perception of others. If the discrepancy involves a behaviour that is critical to your success, we recommend that you initiate a clarification dialogue with the appropriate group of people and/or with your Boss. Consider the following five-step process when conducting such a dialogue:	
Five-step process ☐ *Thank you*	1. Thank them for taking the time to complete the Questionnaire. Identify one or more new insights of your behaviour that came from receiving their feedback.	'I would like to thank you for completing the Questionnaire. One thing I learned is that I'm not as good at listening as I thought.'
☐ *Mention change*	2. Mention one or two changes you initially plan to make as a result of the feedback you received.	'In fact, one specific change I am going to make is to paraphrase what I think I heard.'
☐ *Explain confusion*	3. Explain that some of the information you received was confusing to you, and that you would like their assistance to understand the feedback better.	'However, some of the information I received was confusing to me. I would like to show you that data and get your insights as to what it might mean.'
☐ *Display data*	4. Display the data (use either your actual reports or a copy of selected portions). As you display the data, it maybe necessary to explain the format of the data as you identify the feedback that is confusing to you.	'Specifically, the information about question 3 "Demonstrate consistency between words and actions". As you can see from the data, I believe that I do show consistency and have therefore given myself a high rating. However, you don't seem to agree.'
☐ *Ask questions*	5. Ask questions that attempt to gather additional information. Use a series of 'open questions' (questions that require more than a 'yes' or 'no' response) to discover specific reasons for the discrepancy. Keep the questions focused on *'What more'*, *'What less'* or *'What different'* people desire … not 'Why do you think I am doing poorly?'	'What are some specific situations where my actions don't match my words?' 'Looking back, on what issue would you have liked more consistency between what I said and what I did?'

☐ As we have discussed earlier, do not identify with the report. You are not the originator of the information, so do not be put on the defensive.

☐ Do not be pushed into providing answers. What is important is what the participant thinks, not what you think. Your role is to ask the questions, not answer them.

☐ If you don't know – say so.

A final point on handling conflict: I have found by experience that looking at the report *with* the participant rather than facing them across a table leads to much more collaboration than confrontation.

Don't forget the good news

In most reports there is a mixture of strengths and needs for improvement. It is easy for participants to become obsessed with their perceived weaknesses and to ignore their strong points. It is the facilitator's job to keep the balance.

The high performer

A slightly different issue arises with the person who scores consistently highly throughout the questionnaires. Yes, they do exist! No, they do not achieve their scores through collusion! In reality these people, rare as they are, present an opportunity rather than a threat. The facilitator does not have to rack their brains thinking of significant discrepancies or areas of weakness to talk about. You do not need to think very hard of ways to keep the conversation going. There are four good reasons for this.

First, high performers set their own standards. What to ordinary mortals might be a very high score on an individual item might, to the high performer, be their weakest point. I can assure you that they take this very seriously. High performers are driven by a need to achieve and improve, so any area that scores lower than the others will be a matter of concern to them.

Second, high performers thrive on feedback. Thus a discussion with such a person can be almost guaranteed to result in plans for improvement and further action.

Third, you can discuss with the high performer how they can develop a role in the organisation as a mentor.

Fourth, as an extension of point three, high performers (if in positions of management) will rarely have a team of equally high calibre. This is not deliberate policy on their part. It is more to do with the law of averages and how talent and ability are distributed. It is inevitable, then, that some of their team will not perform as well as they do. Therefore, the top person has a most important role in bringing the performance of their people up to their own high standards, either as coach or role model.

Know when to stop

No one can solve all their performance problems in one session. People need time, sometimes lots of it, to come to terms with, internalise, prioritise and plan action on 360-degree feedback information. For many people it will be the first time they have found out what others think of them. Much of the information will be favourable. Some will not. You will reach a point in most one-to-one sessions where you realise that nothing will be gained at the moment by further debate. At this point you should stop to allow the participant to carry on the process by themselves.

I recently conducted a facilitation session with a senior manager from a large organisation. Over a period of two hours we went through every question, and he had a reason or an argument for each one. The debate was conducted in a very civilised way, but I realised that nothing would be gained by further discussion, at least not at that time. A few days later I heard from one of his colleagues of a meeting he addressed where he extolled the virtues of 360-degree feedback and identified areas where he intended to change.

Twenty-one ways of avoiding feedback

Over the course of conducting individual feedback sessions it becomes possible to identify the different ways in which people seek to avoid facing up to uncomfortable feedback. This is not to denigrate the positive, constructive response which many participants show. However, others give objections that tend to fall into patterns:

Denial/resignation In other words 'I hold my hands up. It is not my fault. There is nothing I can do about this feedback'.

Examples of comments:

- ☐ I didn't understand the question.
- ☐ The questions do not relate to my job.
- ☐ They don't know me well enough.
- ☐ It was answered late at night.
- ☐ I never said that.
- ☐ I'm afraid this is me.
- ☐ I am what I am.
- ☐ I haven't got the time to talk about this right now.

Attack Either the questionnaire, the respondents, or the process:

- ☐ I don't get on with these people.
- ☐ The questions are ambiguous.
- ☐ The last time I did this I got a better result.
- ☐ There must be a mistake in the scanning process.
- ☐ The questionnaire was too long.
- ☐ The questionnaire was too short.
- ☐ I do wish Personnel wouldn't keep dreaming these things up.
- ☐ I've been set up.

Rationalise In other words, try to explain the feedback away:

- ☐ I knew this all along.
- ☐ My respondents did not understand the questions in the same way that I did.
- ☐ The reason for this score is ...
- ☐ Fine, but I can't action this because ...
- ☐ I agree with the feedback.

There is no guaranteed way of dealing with any of these objections. Some facilitators might want to produce arguments against each one. This can work provided that the participant is just exhibiting an initial reaction which one hopes will soon give way to more constructive thought. Unfortunately, the danger of rational counter-arguments in what may be an emotional situation is that they produce a counter-reaction, leading to more arguments and more denial of the feedback. Certainly, it is possible to have ready an answer to each of these objections, but providing them can mean playing into the participant's hands and moving the debate into a safer area for them.

Here is another strategy. Respond politely to objections. Answer some, but do not seek to win the argument every time. Do not get upset or defensive. Wait until the participant has exhausted their objections, and then invite them to start looking at the data.

If this shows signs of going on for too long, an alternative strategy is to give the participant some feedback that describes what they are doing. I do not put the following forward as a fail-safe defuser (it could work the other way), but some participants do respond to this:

'I have noticed that there are several ways in which people respond to their feedback. Some ask a lot of questions, some dive straight into the detail, some spend a lot of time talking about other things. There are many ways to avoid talking about the feedback itself, and that's where I think we are. Let's try to look at the detail. For example, let us look at Question 29.'

Facilitating team 360-degree feedback

In Chapter 3 I described how 360-degree feedback can be applied to teams. The way in which such situations are facilitated is somewhat different from individual sessions, although many of the principles are the same. Here are some of the main variants.

Facilitating individual team member skills

Some systems exist for helping a person to understand how their fellow team members see them demonstrating team skills such as supporting, agreeing, helping, providing information, coaching and so on. These replace the more traditional methods where, for example, team-mates fill up a flipchart with adjectives that describe the individual under scrutiny. In these sessions the writing can take place with the individual out of the room, or the individual can actually lead a session and record other people's comments himself. One of the ground rules is that the participant can ask only questions of clarification, ie not argue or disagree with the comments. This method can be successful but it has several drawbacks:

The data is very 'un-confidential' in that everybody sees all of it whether the participant wants this or not. This can be very threatening to the individual and lead to a defensive reaction. It also threatens or destroys anonymity for respondents, leading them sometimes to be guarded in what they say. It is unstructured, ie it produces a series of solely open-ended questions, which can be hard to make sense of. All these factors make the facilitator's job harder, and can make good, lasting results more difficult to achieve.

If, however, data on team members' performance is collected using 360-degree principles, the information is likely to be more detailed, freely-provided, and easier to use. Facilitation of results still needs to take place on a one-to-one basis, but with one difference. The data is used for team-building purposes, therefore the participant needs help in preparing for some sort of team-building event. During this event they should share some of their data and seek clarification. This method is better than the traditional one because the participant has a chance to look at their data beforehand, with expert help, and have time to prepare themselves.

The team's own culture can make feedback facilitation easy or difficult. For example, having had their feedback reports beforehand some teams will spontaneously engage in sharing their data. This is ideal because the facilitator does not need to do anything to stimulate the activity. All they have to do is keep an eye open to prevent matters getting out of hand. In effect though, the team is pulling the facilitator along, which is much better than the reverse situation. Nevertheless, some teams need much more help to break the ice. A good tip is to persuade the team leader to share their data first. This sets a good example and shows that the team leader is taking the session seriously. It therefore makes it easier for team members to follow suit. Another technique for less forthcoming teams is not to do the feedback sharing in the full group, but to get people in twos or threes. This makes it more likely that people will open up.

Facilitating team data

As we have seen, the team itself can be made the object of 360-degree feedback. This can be done by averaging everyone's individual scores, or by obtaining comments on such issues as team processes, or results as seen by team members or even customers. It differs very much from individual data. Whereas previously everyone got their own individual report, now everybody gets the same report, ie on how the team is viewed as a whole. This can make the task of the facilitator easier, because no individual needs to feel singled out in any way and the team can therefore get more quickly to the task of producing an action plan for improvement. However, you do need to take the precaution of taking the team leader through the results privately beforehand. If anyone is going to feel threatened, this is the person. The team leader *is* the team and therefore needs to feel familiar and comfortable with the information.

As with individual team member facilitation, breaking the team into smaller groups to develop ideas for improvements in team effectiveness is a useful idea. Instead of participating, the team leader can become an extra facilitator for this session.

However, facilitator beware! On some occasions I have presented data to the team only to receive reactions like:

☐ We chose the wrong people.
☐ They can't mean that!
☐ They don't understand.

Have we been here before?

Facilitator training

Internal and external facilitators are usually drawn from the ranks of the human resources, training or psychology professions. The reasons for this are obvious. All are concerned with the study of people and human behaviour. Many experienced practitioners possess advanced facilitation skills. Many have already been through training in occupational and personality testing. Such qualifications make them obvious candidates for conversion to 360-degree feedback facilitation.

However, an organisation looking for potential facilitators should also look at its line management population. Many are surprised at the aptitude some of its line managers show in this area. Clearly, the training needs to take account of a different starting point, but it can be very worthwhile.

It is essential that every trainee facilitator completes and receives feedback on the instrument(s) which they are to use. It is vital to experience what other participants will experience in terms of the questions, the administration, the report layout, but above all the range of emotions felt when they are presented with feedback which may be surprising or expected, and good news or not-so-good news. If possible, they should receive feedback shortly before formal training so that the reflection process has time to start.

In Table 16 there is a simple two-day training timetable.

Table 16

TIMETABLE

Day 1	
8:30	Introduction from the company
	Introduction of participants
	What is all-round feedback?
	360-degree feedback v other assessment methods in use
	Design and validation of the instrument
10:30	*Break*
11:00	Processing and quality control
	Understanding reports
12:00	Action planning
12:30	*Lunch*
1:30	Cases for analysis
3:00	Feedback
3:30	*Break*
4:00	The feedback session
5:00	Briefing for role plays, including homework
Day 2	
8:30	Introduction and re-cap
9:00	Warm up
9:20	Feedback
9:45	Introduction to role plays
10:00	*Break*
10:15	Session 1: A Facilitator. B Participant. C Observer
11:15	Feedback
11:30	Session 2: A Observer. B Facilitator. C Participant
12:30	*Lunch*
1:30	Session 3: A Participant. B Observer. C Facilitator
2:30	Feedback and review
3:00	Further thoughts on action planning and implementation
4:00	Sharing feedback with others
	Close

Aids to interpretation and action-planning

The attitudes both of user organisations and instrument suppliers vary widely when it comes to providing non-facilitated help to feedback recipients. At the one extreme are those who say that no interpretation or solution should be suggested; what is needed is expert one-to-one facilitation, followed by action-planning, followed by support for self-development provided by the organisation. Others argue that it is better to give much more help and guidance by providing interpretation and pre-scribing solutions. Interpretation can be provided by means of expert systems and solutions offered automatically, consisting of which course to attend or which book to read. While respecting this as a means of helping a few people I must confess to pre-ferring a more fundamental approach. I believe that the process of trying to arrive at your own understanding of the feedback, and working out your own action plan will result in much more solidly-based learning. This is more likely to produce perma-nent, observable changes of behaviour in the workplace than if understanding and solutions are presented on a plate.

Sometimes, however, a little outside help (in addition to that provided by the facilitator) can start a person off on the right road. Table 17 contains an extract from a commentary which some organisations provide for participants when they receive their feedback report. You will notice, however, that it does not interpret; it points the participants in a certain direction and

Table 17

EXTRACT FROM A COMMENTARY

Strictly private and confidential

Dear <Particpant Name>.

360-degree feedback

I have pleasure in enclosing your personal feedback report based on the questionnaire you and your respondents completed recently. To assist you in interpreting the findings I have prepared a special commentary which I hope you will find useful.

Just to remind you first of all, the questionnaire consisted on 45 multiple-choice questions. The answer choices available on a five-point scale were:

   1 = *To a very limited extent*

   2 = *To a limited extent*

3 = *To a moderate extent*
4 = *To a great extent*
5 = *To a very great extent*

There was also a space to mark if you were unable to answer the question.

Finally, there were six open-ended questions in which respondents were asked to describe particularly good performance, and areas for change.

Profile and analysis report
Part One

This is your highest-rated area overall, with an average rating of 4.50. You have achieved a very high rating for Q1, 'behave honestly and ethically in all business situations', and the Ags. of 0.76 indicates a high degree of agreement among your respondents. Well done! At the other end of the spectrum Q10, 'support a balance between work and personal lives', is an area that you should consider a priority development need. There are some comments relating to this in the open-ended section that you may find useful. Also, there is a low-rated cluster of questions relating to listening to others and using their feedback (Q12, Q7 and Q6). These questions are all linked and, as such, they can be worked on together. An improvement effort in one will impact in effect across all linked areas. Finally, Q8, 'encourage others to develop their skills and abilities', would benefit from an improvement effort. How can *you* develop your skills and abilities in this area?

Part Two

Your average rating under this heading is 3.25. You have achieved an excellent score for Q13, 'demonstrate commitment to meeting or exceeding customer requirements'. Congratulations! There are also a number of behaviours that require attention in this section. Your lowest rated question is Q21, 'support others in taking prudent risks'. Also, Q18 is low-rated. Think of someone you consider to be excellent at conflict resolution and observe them carefully in relevant situations. How does their behaviour differ from your own? You may also want to spend some time thinking about how you can provide clear goals and direction for others (Q17). Lastly, try to explore new ways of recognising team accomplishments (Q19).

Part Three

This is your lowest rated section overall, with an average rating of 3.17. You have achieved some very high scores in the area of personal achievement (Q28, Q29 and Q30). Well done! However, there is a low-rated cluster of questions relating to dealing with other people's performance (Q27, Q26 and Q25). What can you do to become more effective in this area? Also, there is a low-rated cluster of questions concerning vision and forward thinking (Q35, Q34 and Q36) that you may want to turn your attention to. Finally, try to think about how you can balance the needs of customers, employees and the business when making decisions (Q32).

asks them questions. NB: Commentaries like these are designed to be read in conjunction with the feedback report, rather than to replace it. This example does not include the actual report. The reader should look instead at the overall approach used in the commentary.

The next step along this road might be a self-development guide an extract of which appears in Table 18. The purpose of

Table 18

COACHING SELF-DEVELOPMENT

Question 38   Coach their people

Your respondents (usually subordinates but occasionally others) think you should take more time to develop their effectiveness. There are two ways you can do this: take *time out*, ie set aside time for coaching sessions, or make a *secondary use of time* already allocated for other activities.

Time out: try to find a short period of time (say one hour) every week or fort-night to devote to improving your subordinates' effectiveness. You can use it to:

- ☐ give informal appraisals
- ☐ give feedback
- ☐ discuss delegated tasks
- ☐ answer questions
- ☐ share insights on tasks, issues or people
- ☐ coach on specific tasks or projects
- ☐ teach specific skills
- ☐ discuss examples of what has gone right or wrong.

This can be done with one subordinate or with several together. But the danger is that other priorities intervene and the intervals between sessions get longer and longer. If this does happen, then you may have done more harm than good, because the expectations of your staff have been initially raised but subsequently dashed.

The second way is to use current activities (projects, meetings, and other business situations) to maximum advantage by extracting from the situation a learning opportunity. There are numerous ways you can do this. For example, if you attend a meeting with a subordinate, spend five minutes afterwards on a quick post-mortem of what was said, what happened etc. If your subordinate presents you with a report, make sure you go over it with them and discuss different or better ways in which the information could have been presented. Let subordinates give part of a presentation that you are to give, and then provide feedback afterwards. The main things you need in order to use this option are the willingness to develop your staff on the job, and the ability to spot opportunities to do it. If you can do both these then there are untold opportunities for developing others' effectiveness.

this particular version is to clarify the question, suggest a few possible interpretations, and give some tips on what to do. You will notice though that it is still not very prescriptive. However, aids like this should be used in conjunction with one-to-one facilitation rather than as a substitute for it.

Action-planning

Action planning involves converting our understanding of the feedback into a written commitment to action. Essentially the participant should be planning two types of action: behaviour and development shown on the action-planning pro-forma which follows.

Behaviour

This type of action plan involves identifying a behaviour that is not carried out often enough, or well enough. The participant then plans what they will do to exhibit this behaviour more. The key point is to decide how this behaviour will be displayed and under what circumstances, including the type of respondent group that has identified it.

The following is a useful action planning format for such behaviours.

List 1 (Table 19) – strengths I can contribute On this list the participant writes their main strengths, together with how they can use these to benefit others.

Table 19

LIST I – STRENGTHS I CAN CONTRIBUTE

Behaviours identified as my strengths	How can I use these to benefit others' performance
Critical thinking Particularly 'Seeing the big picture in a mass of detail'.	1. In discussion with others identify situations where we are starting to get lost in the details, and summarise what I see as the main strategic issues.
'Dealing with the causes of problems rather than the symptoms'.	2. In talking to colleagues, help them understand the difference between the concepts of cause and effect.

List 2 (Table 20) – areas I can develop List 2 is a working sheet to help the participant devise a plan for resolving development areas.

Table 20

LIST 2 – AREAS I CAN DEVELOP

Behaviours to develop	Response group
1. Demonstrate a consistent commitment to quality	1. Staff
15. Contribute effectively to meetings	15. Peers
23. Contribute outside their own technical area	23. Peers
16. Negotiate differences of opinion openly and fairly	16. Peers
19. Demonstrate confidence in their own technical abilities	19. Peers and Boss
33. Develop realistic plans for reaching goals	33. Staff

List 3 (Table 21) – priority areas I want to improve

Table 21

LIST 3 – PRIORITY AREAS I WANT TO IMPROVE

Behaviours to develop	Priority
1. Demonstrate a consistent commitment to quality	1. Medium
15. Contribute effectively to meetings	15. High
23. Contribute outside their own technical area	23. High
16. Negotiate differences of opinion openly and fairly	16. Medium
19. Demonstrate confidence in their own technical abilities	19. High
33. Develop realistic plans for reaching goals	33. Low

List 4 (Table 22) – action plan – top three or four items to be changed and my plans to make it happen This list, when completed, becomes the action sheet for the participant.

Table 22

LIST 4 – ACTION PLAN – TOP 3/4 ITEMS TO BE CHANGED AND MY PLANS TO MAKE IT HAPPEN

Behaviour	Specifically what will I do differently?	Help/support available
15. Contribute effectively to meetings 23. Contribute outside own speciality	I will make sure that at the regular XYZ meeting with peers I make at least one comment on each agenda item – whatever the subject.	When the agenda is sent out I will identify any items where I understand very little, and ask a colleague what they mean.

Making action plans work

You may have noticed in the examples shown that (other than a heading 'Help/support available') there is no mention of training or development. The reason is that an action plan should concentrate on just that! In other words it should describe what you are going to do differently, when, and with whom! 360-degree feedback lends itself very much to this approach because of the specific way in which the behaviours are worded. Very often, the knowledge that it is a weak area together with the ability to identify opportunities to behave differently, are enough for a change of behaviour to be planned – and observed.

Here are two more ideas for making it all happen:

Show your action plan to a colleague and invite them to challenge it. If you need help and advice, ask them.

In some cases it is a good idea to signal to colleagues in advance that you will be acting a little differently in some areas. A sudden, unexplained change in what you say or do can be unsettling or confusing if people do not know why you are doing it. The solution is to share parts of your action plan with colleagues so that they know what to expect. Thus you might say to your reports:

'In my feedback report many of you identified delegation as an area I should improve. In order to make this work best I intend to talk to each of you individually over the next few weeks. We will discuss how much authority you think you are able to cope with, and to discuss your development needs. I also intend to be more specific, when asking you to do tasks, about precisely how I will measure successful completion of them.'

Development plans

In my view a development plan and an action plan are two different documents, with different purposes. As we have seen above, an action plan is what you are going to do to implement a change in behaviour. It can be very specific, detailing the circumstances in which you will apply it. However, there will be some circumstances where this by itself is not enough. Some skills need to be explored, taught, learned and practised before they are used for real. These activities should be part of the development plan. Items that you would expect to see on this would be:

- [ ] skill or competency to be developed
- [ ] learning method to be used
- [ ] other people involved (eg mentors or coaches)
- [ ] standards of performance required
- [ ] target date for completion.

Self-evaluation check-list for facilitating one-to-one feedback

- [ ] Do I prepare adequately?
- [ ] Do I communicate the purpose of the feedback?
- [ ] Do I explain my role?
- [ ] Do I explain the purpose of the session?
- [ ] Do I agree a timescale?
- [ ] How do I start the discussion?
- [ ] Do I make sure the participant takes responsibility for their own feedback?

☐ What is my predominant facilitation style – present, clarify, persuade, coach?

☐ Is this appropriate?

☐ How good am I at achieving a focus on detail as opposed to generalities?

☐ How well do I achieve a focus on priority areas?

☐ How good am I at helping participants to seek clarification from others?

☐ How well do I handle conflict?

☐ Do I know when to stop?

☐ Can I identify and deal with feedback avoidance?

☐ How effectively do I help participants to convert needs into action plans and development plans?

8

PLANNING AND IMPLEMENTING A 360-DEGREE FEEDBACK PROJECT

Discipline and focused awareness ... contribute to the act of creation.
John Poppy

Quite as important as legislation is vigilant oversight of administration.
Woodrow Wilson

Key points

The stages in implementing a 360-degree feedback project are:

- [ ] Learn about the subject by research, experimentation and piloting.
- [ ] Establish purpose and end result. This can mean revisiting the analysis done when designing the questionnaire and making sure that the various layers of objectives are still valid.
- [ ] Identify project steps. These will consist of design, piloting, validation, decisions about data collection and processing, post-assessment support and rollout.
- [ ] Establish roles particularly those of participants and respondents, the boss, the facilitator, the project manager and the champion.
- [ ] Identify and implement project controls, particularly identifying pitfalls and making sure that a benchmark of best practice is understood by all parties.
- [ ] Create organisational learning, in other words make sure that the lessons learned from the project are not forgotten, and are available for use either later in this project or

Many people who engage in 360-degree feedback sometimes realise too late that there is more to it than at first meets the eye. Organisations that have tried to implement it quickly, on a large-scale basis, without proper preparation, often find themselves in trouble. Basically they underestimate the amount of learning that has to take place within the organisation. This chapter presents a more considered approach.

Learning about the subject
This means finding out about the subject by researching it, experimentation and piloting.

Research
Reading: this book is one of only a handful of full-length treatments of the subject. There are, however, a growing number of shorter publications, papers, articles, etc starting to appear in the UK. The more useful ones give examples of what other organisations have done. Other articles have appeared more frequently in the USA, but conditions there are not quite the same, and some of the issues need to be treated differently. A short reading list of current publications appears at the end of this chapter.

Benchmarking: several organisations are quite happy to share their experiences. Some projects are now quite well known, and provide a useful source of learning for the less experienced.

Talking to test publishers and consultants: as 360-degree feedback becomes more popular, the number of external organisations offering services becomes more numerous. This is to be expected, but organisations are already offering quite different services. The complete range of 360-degree feedback services that you can acquire from outside the organisation is:

- supply of standard test instruments
- processing of standard instruments
- adaptation of standard instruments
- customised questionnaire design

☐ processing of your own in-house instrument
☐ supply of standard instruments that include their own software
☐ software-only supply and implementation
☐ software design
☐ facilitation
☐ training in facilitation skills, questionnaire design, software use, general 360-degree feedback appreciation
☐ project management
☐ consultancy advice on any of the above aspects.

Some firms specialise in many aspects, some in a limited number. Not many can offer the full range of products and services.

Experimentation

This is the point at which someone has to 'get their feet wet'; individuals try out some aspects of 360-degree feedback either on themselves or on others. The purpose of the experiment is to decide whether the organisation is going to invest in the technique, and to give pointers on what direction it should follow. It is a good idea for those who will be sponsoring the project to be involved at the experimentation stage. This usually means some members of senior management, and the human resources function. In this subject area nothing is so convincing as speaking from experience.

The cheapest and least risky way to dip a toe into the water is to try out some of the standard instruments that are available. These include a large number covering management and leadership, but also those that deal more specifically with internal consultancy, team skills and selling. The range of report formats available is very wide.

Some experiments lead to the organisation adopting the technique on a wider basis – others do not. The ones that do seem to have a distinguishing characteristic. They tend to involve situations where a department – be it human resources, quality, or sales – has deliberately set out to find out about 360-degree feedback in a measured way, for example by a systematic search of the literature or by talking to research institutions, specialist consultants, or other users. The ones that are less likely to go forward are those where the research has been the private initiative of one individual, who has perhaps designed their own instrument and uses more basic processes and technology.

The message is clear: if you want to take the best informed decision on this, be comprehensive in your research and systematic in your experimentation.

Piloting

Piloting perhaps more properly belongs as a stage of the project once it is underway. By now the organisation has decided to invest in 360-degree feedback on a medium to large scale. However, there is still a lot of learning to be done and very many decisions to take, as we shall see later. Piloting was covered in more detail in Chapter 5, so all we need say now is that it is intended as a prelude to large-scale implementation. Its aim is to test out or 'de-bug' as many aspects of the final system as possible, including the questions, the scale, the report format, processing, administration and facilitation.

Establish purpose and result

Remember that 360-degree feedback is not an end in itself; it is a performance measurement device. Like other methods of measuring performance, it can have several uses. It is dangerous not to think out in advance the precise reasons for wanting to use it. If these are not defined and communicated clearly to those who will be affected, then the latter will supply their own reasons. Many people, as we know, see any departure from the *status quo* as a threat. The idea of receiving feedback from people other than your boss can seem strange, or an attack on the established order of things. Unless people are able to understand through careful communication why it is to be implemented then rumours will fly: redundancies, downsizing, demotion, 'unwarranted interference by an asylum of psychologists in my right to manage' – the list of misconceptions is long. Knowing why you want to implement it and communicating this will not eliminate the list, but it will certainly reduce it. Also, in Chapter 3 we looked at the differing degrees of risk associated with the applications of 360-degree feedback. Now is the time to start looking at these implications.

In Chapter 4 we looked at the different layers of objectives relating to 360-degree feedback design. Again, there is no need to dwell on these, other than to give another example. This one is from a Franco-British hi-tech company:

Overall objective

☐ to improve the style of management in our company.

Specific objectives

☐ to create a more open, democratic culture
☐ to balance the management by objectives system introduced recently with attention to management processes, ie *how* people achieve their results
☐ to improve the way in which employees give and receive feedback.

Other layers of objectives

☐ to introduce 360-degree feedback to improve the annual appraisal meeting
☐ to implement 360-degree feedback to our top 200 managers, followed by the next 300
☐ to decide following this whether to introduce it to the whole of our 5,000-strong workforce.

This company has clearly worked out what it wants to achieve and the subsidiary objectives involved. This will make the planning much easier.

Identify and define the project stages

The main stages which follow the setting of objectives – design, piloting, validation, decisions about data collection and processing, post-assessment support, and rollout – are generic to any 360-degree feedback project, and most have been discussed already in this book. However, their length and complexity will vary according to the nature of the organisation and the type of project. One important lesson that organisations should be aware of (preferably in advance!) is that it is very easy to under-estimate the time involved in any of the stages. In addition to all the usual events which bedevil projects – such as changes of key personnel, reorganisations, and timetable clashes with other initiatives – there are some specific ones to look out for. For example, in questionnaire design and validation here are some potential causes of delay:

☐ the organisation decides to re-examine the competency framework
☐ the initial group of people you ask for feedback on your first draft of items does not confine itself to this but insists on rewriting the first draft in committee
☐ there are difficulties in getting the first pilot group together on one date, so you need to have several meetings instead
☐ someone discover that the pilot groups are not representa-tive of the target population so further groups have to be set up
☐ questionnaire returns from the pilot groups take four weeks to come in rather than the intended two weeks
☐ there are delays in approving revisions.

Although many of these delays may only be short, their accu-mulation can result in project completion dates being missed by wide margins. This is particularly so when the completion has to coincide with other events in the corporate calendar, such as launching the rollout at the annual management con-ference (having announced it in advance) or missing the annual performance review and having to wait until the cycle comes round again.

One of the most important aspects of a project, one which can make or break it, is the ability and willingness of those in charge of it to communicate the purpose and the detail at the right time. The right time may differ according to circum-stances, but it is usually at an early stage followed by regular updates. The organisation needs to plan very carefully what its communication strategy will be. There are many ways of using existing communication systems to promote and explain what you have in mind. Company newsletters, management conferences, and communication groups can be used, together with special events.

Just as important, if not more so, is talking to individuals, whether they are influential in the organisation or not, and trying to resolve individual concerns. It is not possible to anticipate all concerns, but the main ones are predictable. It is a good idea to have answers available. Here are some objections which can be met in advance or at the time they are raised, together with a possible response.

'People can secure good results by choosing friends as respondents'

This point was answered earlier. There is no evidence to suggest that friends will score you favourably. Indeed the combination of guaranteed anonymity and their concern for your success might cause them to be harder on you.

'I don't think we're ready for this yet'

The smart answer to this is 'If you were really ready then you wouldn't need it'. In other words, an organisation in which there was free communication, where managers were judged on process rather than just results, and where people welcomed and were prepared to act on accurate behaviour feedback, might not need 360-degree feedback. The chances are, though, that they would be using it already in some shape or form. The technique is meant for organisations who are not 'ready' in that it can make their feedback processes better and employees' confidence in them greater. Organisations whose culture is not ready may indeed have to think carefully about how they implement 360-degree feedback, but if the project is well managed then they can obtain significant results.

'But I already talk to my staff and get feedback from them'

Of course most managers talk to their staff. Some even ask for feedback. But in a face-to-face situation just how honest and direct are people prepared to be? Do we deal with our own bosses in such a way? How specific are we? Managers who already talk to their staff are well placed to take the dialogue to a much greater value-level by using this technique.

'We will all disappear under a mountain of paperwork'

This again has been covered already. In practice it does not seem to happen, but organisations can take safeguards to prevent it, for example by carefully planning the rollout of a project, by monitoring the overuse of individuals as respondents, or by looking at other data collection methods.

'Some people will never change, whatever feedback they get' Some people make a habit of ignoring advice or feedback whether it comes from a friend, their accountant or their doctor. Yet do not underestimate the power of this technique to give surprises or to focus people on areas that they were aware of but have not been inclined to change. Remember also the power of peer pressure, both from the point of view of peer feedback, and because colleagues in the organisation are going through the same process as well.

'People (like me) who are already self-aware do not need extra feedback'
Self awareness is an essential ingredient for change, but by itself it does not create performance improvement. People who are self-aware will receive fewer surprises, and they will know their areas for development as well as their strengths. However, it might come as a surprise to learn that your colleagues are as aware of your shortcomings as you are, and therefore provide more motivation to do something about the results.

'How can you prove that it really works?'
By pointing to other organisations who have used it successfully, by carrying out proper validation, and by re-testing. Scientific proof is available if we are prepared to obtain it.

'When it gets round to re-testing time people will deliberately change their style to influence the results'
So what? The purpose of this technique *is* to get people to change their behaviour. It might be better if the new style came from an innately-felt desire to change, rather than an external influence such as embarrassment caused by negative results from a re-test, or perhaps a smaller bonus. Nevertheless, it is a change.

A more telling question would be: 'How effectively will this produce permanent change?' The answer is that it depends on all the factors that you would expect to see in an organisation development project: clear objectives, good design, achieving buy-in, communication, excellent planning, and effective monitoring of results with determined follow-up. In that sense there is no difference between 360-degree feedback and any other organisational change project.

Establish roles and responsibilities

Participants and respondents

Decisions are clearly needed on who will be the participants and respondents. Chapters 1 and 2 cover issues such as how many respondents, what type, and the need to establish rules for selection. The methods of communicating the purpose of the project and the fine detail of what is expected of them need very careful thought.

The boss

We have already seen how the role of the boss changes from simply an evaluator to that of a coach. In an interesting study in the USA, John Keenan, director of leadership programmes at the University of Wisconsin, identified how important are the involvement of the boss and the provision of post-assessment support. The study involved 400 managers in a state government department. A 360-degree feedback leadership questionnaire was used to provide baseline feedback initially. Two groups were created for testing and measurement purposes.

Group 1 received their feedback results in a structured one-day workshop. Participants created written action plans during the session. Within ten days of the workshop participants followed up with their respective bosses to share results and action plans, and to identify and register for any training and development activities required.

Bosses agreed to conduct three follow-up and coaching sessions throughout the year with each participant, to monitor progress, provide suggestions for improvement, and reinforce successes.

Group 2 also attended a structured workshop and developed written action plans which they shared with their bosses ten days afterwards. No follow-up, coaching sessions or training and development activities were included. Feedback was shared with the boss, but with no accountability or next steps identified.

A reassessment took place for both groups one year later.

Group 2 recorded an average overall increase in performance of 22 per cent on each of the 16 competencies tested. The researchers attributed the increase to the more motivated participants within the group, an increased awareness of their strengths and development needs, and a desire to engage in self-directed development.

Group 1 recorded an average overall increase of 67 per cent across the 16 competencies. The researchers attributed this increase to the structured process of participants being held accountable of the results of their actions, taking the initiative to follow up, share, and engage in dialogue with the boss, and to enrol in appropriate training and development activities. The willingness of the boss to provide on-going coaching and support was considered a key factor.

Many bosses cannot be expected to carry out this new role without some degree of training themselves. At the very least, everyone will need a detailed briefing about their role in the process. Some, though, will need more intensive training in the skills of giving feedback and coaching.

The facilitator

We have seen in Chapter 7 that facilitation is a key element in the feedback process, and can influence strongly the value that individuals or the organisation get out of it. The main decision on choice of facilitators is: do we use internal facilitators, external facilitators or a mixture of both?

☐ Internal facilitation is cheaper and perhaps more flexible. However, time and money are involved in selecting facilitators (whether from human resources or line management), and in training and accrediting them. Eventually, and for larger projects, issues of quality control also arise.

☐ External facilitators are usually more expensive, but are of high quality if they come from an outside organisation already known to those managing the project.

Many organisations use a mixture of both approaches, with external people being used for the most senior staff members, for potentially difficult sessions, and for training internal staff. This can leave much of the work in the hands of internal staff, but with the availability of external resources to supplement internal ones.

The project manager

All 360-degree feedback projects require project management from within the organisation. The person selected needs to be able to devote time (not necessarily all their time) to the project, and must also be very committed to the process. They need planning and problem-solving skills, and high degrees of communication, influencing and mediation skills. I have noticed the anxiety that 360-degree feedback can create at all levels within the organisation. Perhaps this is not surprising at junior and middle ranks given the experiences many have had, or seen at second-hand, of down-sizing, delayering, and outsourcing in recent years. Even senior employees have experienced this themselves. In organisations where this climate is common there is bound to be a reaction against yet another form of assessment.

However, senior or more established employees can also react for another reason. In many cases the amount of feedback we receive diminishes as we rise up the organisation. The principal reason is that in traditional management cultures the qualification for giving feedback has tended to be seniority. Clearly then, the higher you are, the fewer people there are who are available or willing to give detailed performance feedback. What feedback there is will have come mainly from the boss and will be focused on results or achievements. This is not a climate which will encourage changes in style or behaviour. It is much more likely to continue reinforcing the *status quo*. Introducing 360-degree feedback, with its use of peers and staff as raters, and its focus on process, can be seen as a threat. I believe, however, that confidentiality and how the data is used may not be the biggest issues here. It could be the threat of finally seeing themselves as others see them, that provides the most discomfort as well as a challenge to their seniority. Someone – namely the project manager – needs to be able to foresee situations like this, and deploy the organisational skills needed to manage them.

The champion

It is a good idea to identify one or more people in the organisation whose degree of influence will enable them to open doors which the project manager or others involved in the project find closed to them. Such a person will usually be in a senior position, will be influential, and will be committed to 360-degree feedback either from past experience or because you have convinced them of its merits. The role of the champion is to use their influence to overcome obstacles which appear in the path of progress. Such a person can come from any department. They may be the voice that speaks for 360-degree feedback at board meetings. They do not need great technical knowledge of the process, nor do they need to be involved in the detail of the project. What they do need is personal commitment and the ability to speak from experience.

Establish and implement project controls

This is not a treatise on project management, and indeed 360-degree feedback projects share many aspects of other organisation development exercises. Elsewhere in this book I have also covered many of the things that the project manager needs to be aware of to prevent the project from getting out of hand or failing. These include potential causes of delay and negative reactions of participants when they receive feedback and facilitation. I do not propose, therefore, to go further into these. However, there are some other issues which are unique and which do merit further discussion, first of some other things which can go wrong, and second of the absence of any official guidelines for best practice.

What could go wrong?

It is not always easy to identify pitfalls in advance, but experience tells us that some 'hiccups' can be avoided through good planning and implementation.

People get cold feet

This is almost certain to happen at some stage in the project, often just before the results are distributed. Those running the project (and their sponsors) need to be ready for this. They need to be ready to reassure and give assurance on confidentiality and the overall value of the feedback.

People react poorly to the results

Inevitably, participants get surprises from the difference between how they see themselves and how others see them. If not properly handled this can lead to rejection of the information, emotional reactions, conceivably a lowering of morale, and a worsening of performance rather than an improvement. Such issues cannot be left to chance. To avoid them you need to provide careful initial consultation and briefing, thoughtful management of expectations, a well-designed questionnaire, and first-class, professional debriefing and facilitation.

Raters hold back from providing frank feedback

This can happen when the prevailing culture of an organisation is either complacent or blame-ridden. Complacency in the organisation about people, results and performance will not lead to respondents taking the process seriously enough. If people do not understand why the project is being carried out and what the results will be used for they will not give it the attention it deserves. Questionnaires, if completed at all, will not be taken seriously and people will not take the trouble to think issues through. Why bother to be honest and accurate? In a blame culture respondents will fear a witch-hunt if they give honest but critical answers. Participants will not want to share their data with others for fear of this being seen as a sign of weakness or of attracting further criticism. Again, careful briefing of respondents, particularly on the aims of the project, the absolute requirement for honest feedback, and issues of confidentiality, is critical. It also helps if those at the top of the organisation are seen practising what they preach and not just paying lip service. Any 360-degree project intended to cover management levels should start at the top. It is not just a matter of setting an example. For the reasons explained earlier in this chapter, senior management may for years have been starved of honest feedback on their own processes and will find it invaluable.

Too much attention to technology

The technology inherent in sophisticated data collection methods, feedback processing and report formats should not be seen as an end in itself, but sometimes it is. Overemphasis on these matters at the expense of the less glamorous issues such as careful planning, detailed communication, sensitive facilitation and appropriate post-assessment support is not a recipe for success.

Flavour of the month

'It's just another craze', 'What will they think of next?' and similar reactions seem almost inevitable in these days of 'initiative overload'. It can lead to many undesirable results, such as this reaction from a boss when shown feedback by an employee who had gone through the process: 'I see that the scores given by your reports are pretty low. I don't know where they get these ideas from and you will see that I have rated you pretty highly. Nothing to worry about then really. I doubt whether we'll have to do this again. It'll be something different next time.'

The way to prevent or minimise this type of reaction is to carry out, as described previously, all stages of the project professionally – and then to stick to it and see it through. Do not surrender or modify the technique at the first whiff of a hostile reaction. Listening to and understanding reactions are important, but so are having confidence in the techniques and being determined to see them through.

Best practice

In order properly to control a 360-degree feedback project there has to exist in the minds of those managing it a set of principles and standards which, if followed, give confidence that the project is well-founded in theory and practice.

If asked to define the term 'best practice' I would say that it is:

> A comprehensive code of professional conduct which is to be followed in a given area, is defined authoritatively by acknowledged experts who work in that area, and is generally seen as what everyone must strive to do.

Within the field of 360-degree feedback there is not yet a best practice code which meets this definition. Help is at hand, however. Here is an extract from an article written by my colleagues Lorenza Clifford and Harvey Bennett and published by The British Psychological Society in its journal *Selection and Development Review*, Volume 13 No 2, in April 1997:

Common practice is *not* best practice

Best practice is a widely misunderstood concept. There are best practice guides on many subjects that cover only common practice. They are useful as guides to what others do, but their titles are misleading. Readers are left with the idea that following what others have done will ensure success.

An illustration of this point is the use of personality assessment in selection. Best practice is under constant review and new research pushes forward our thinking. Common practice lags behind the current thinking on best practice, while some common practices are frankly pretty awful ... some of it sampled first hand! The codes of practice that we have seen in the area of occupational testing have typically been of high quality, with an emphasis on 'best' rather than 'common'.

The issues are as complex with 360-degree feedback as they are with other forms of occupational assessment. Purpose and context play a very important role in deciding what instrument should be used, with whom and how. 360-degree feedback has a shorter history in the UK than other forms of assessment and as a result there has been considerably less debate about its construction and application.

As with conventional forms of assessment, the information gathered is very sensitive. According to a survey by the Industrial Society in 1995, one-third of their sample of 800 organisations identified that the main obstacle to implementing a 360-degree feedback was that people felt threatened by it.

In recognition of the sensitivity of traditional assessment information, professional bodies, such as The British Psychological Society and the Institute of Personnel and Development, have issued codes of conduct, backed up by professional qualifications and a certification scheme. However, there are some points specific to 360-degree feedback where the nationally agreed guidelines for conventional occupational testing do not give specific guidance to users and adequate protection to participants and respondents against poor practice. This is especially problematic as there are no official accreditation requirements for users and facilitators of 360-degree feedback either specifically or under the umbrella of existing Occupational Testing qualifications.

Objectives of applying best practice

☐ Ethics: handling data and feedback sensitively, maintaining trust and informed usage.

☐ Efficiency: smooth running of each programme, reliability of data and proper consideration of communication issues.

☐ Effectiveness: optimisation of the results, making use of strategic data, getting value for money.

Best practice guidelines

The list of responsibilities below is a starting point for a discussion on 'best practice' and is designed to provide clients and colleagues with some specific guidelines to follow in their use of 360-degree feedback instruments in the absence of a nationally recognised, authoritative standard.

☐ Examine the range of 360-degree feedback providers and ensure that the one chosen is *qualified* to advise on 'best practice'.

☐ Ensure that the 360-degree feedback instrument chosen is *appropriate* for the purpose.

☐ Evaluate the information provided for standard instruments to ensure *justification* for use.

☐ Ensure that, *without exception*, participants are helped to understand their feedback by a qualified internal or external facilitator.

☐ Obtain the necessary *training* and ensure that no unqualified person is allowed to administer the instrument.

☐ Give *feedback* information to the instrument provider to enable the quality of their instruments and service to be improved continuously.

☐ Respect copyright and data protection *laws*.

☐ Strive to answer participants' questions and provide them with accurate *information*, or to pass them on to someone who can.

☐ Arrange for an independent, qualified person to answer participants' and respondents' *questions/complaints* in confidence and make these arrangements known.

☐ Explain clearly and honestly to participants and respondents the *extent of confidentiality*, ie who will see the completed questionnaires and the feedback reports, how they will be used, and then stick to your word.

☐ Use an instrument according to its purpose and in line with the *recommended strategy*.

☐ Only use an instrument for a different purpose after *careful examination* of the implications.

- ☐ Ensure that feedback is *accurate* and imparted to the participant in a *sensitive* manner.
- ☐ Ensure that the *implications* of the feedback are understood by the participant and so avoid a 'so what?' reaction.
- ☐ Encourage participants to make *specific action plans* and prioritise their development efforts.
- ☐ *Respect* and help the individual regardless of the desirability of their feedback profile.
- ☐ Encourage participants to *share* their feedback and action plans with their boss and colleagues.
- ☐ Never reveal the content of a participant's feedback report unless that participant has *specifically agreed* that you may do so.
- ☐ Evaluate the use of 360-degree instruments to ensure their *utility* within your organisation/department.
- ☐ Ensure that those people using the information from a 360-degree feedback process are aware of its *shelf life*.
- ☐ If a breach of these guidelines occurs, take appropriate action or bring it to the attention of someone who can.

Evaluate and create organisational learning

One company recently sent me a questionnaire for comment. They are in the middle of a large-scale project and are now at a stage where, having implemented it in their management structures, they wish to begin implementing it further down the organisation. They had previously used outside help for developing the first questionnaire they used. On the second in-house version, the design did not seem to meet many of the guidelines described in Chapter 4. This surprised me because their own staff had been closely involved in the project and should have learned more than they obviously had. When discussing this we finally realised why. The project manager for the first phase had left the company and had been replaced. The second manager had taken over, but at the implementation stage, and had not been involved at the design stage. Unfortunately, the initial learning had not remained within the organisation.

This is a small but telling example of how the lessons from 360-degree projects can be lost, even in cases where those involved adopt the highest standards of professionalism.

Evaluation of the project at the appropriate stage should produce a lot of useful information. However, the results should not be confined to a small band of people. They need to be broadcast as much as possible so that the lessons are not forgotten. For example, in addition to data about how the questionnaire was received and how people have changed, an organisation can learn a lot about its reaction to change, and how it manages projects.

Check-list for planning and implementing a 360-degree feedback project

- ☐ Am I satisfied that sufficient organised research, experimentation and piloting have been done?
- ☐ Am I, and are others, clear on the purpose and objectives of the project?
- ☐ Have the following project stages been planned:
  design
  piloting
  validation
  data collection
  processing
  post-assessment support
  rollout?
- ☐ Have I allowed enough time for the stages?
- ☐ What are the possible causes of delay?
- ☐ Have I timed the communication and launch to fit in with other events and processes?
- ☐ Have I set up and communicated the various roles properly to participants?
  respondents?
  bosses?
  facilitators?
  champion?
- ☐ What project controls have I set up?
- ☐ How will I measure the project against best practice?
- ☐ How will I review the project to make sure that the lessons are learned?

References and further reading

CLIFFORD L. *and* BENNETT, H. (1997) 'Best Practice in 360° Feedback'. *Selection and Development Review*. Vol. 13, No. 2. April.

FRANCE, S. *360° Appraisal*. London, The Industrial Society, 1997.

HARDY L., DEVINE M. *and* HEATH L. *Feedback – 'Unguided Missile or Powerful Weapon?* Ashridge Management Group, 1996.

THE INDUSTRIAL SOCIETY. *Managing Best Practice: The regular benchmark 360° Appraisal*. London, The Industrial Society, 1995.

KETTLEY P. *Personal Feedback: Cases in point*. London, The Institute for Employment Studies 1997.

Part III

THE FUTURE

9

THE FUTURE

Some people think the future means the end of history. They're wrong. We haven't run out of history quite yet.

Captain James T. Kirk, Stardate 9523.8

Key points

☐ Possible future applications of 360-degree feedback include remuneration, strategic organisational analysis and as an aid to creating open cultures.

☐ Some organisations will bring 360-degree processes in-house, and the role of external providers may change.

☐ The technique will be linked with other systems to create integrated human resources applications.

☐ New parts of the organisation will experience 360-degree feedback, but not all.

☐ Technology will be a major driver of progress in 360-degree feedback, particularly the development of artificial intelligence.

☐ Don't forget the health warning!

In the UK 360-degree feedback has achieved prominence only in the last two years or so. Before that it was used by a relatively small number of organisations. In the rest of Western Europe the technique does not yet appear to be at the forefront of people's thinking but it is certainly not unknown. In the USA it has been in existence for a long time, but again has only come into widespread use in recent years. We are therefore talking about a technique that is still in its infancy as far as most organisations are concerned. For many people it has no track record and is therefore unproven. It may turn out to be short lived or it may achieve a permanent place in the armoury of techniques available for measuring performance. The only certainty is that it will change.

The other parts of this book describe the background and theories behind 360-degree feedback, how to apply it, and how other organisations are actually using it. Most of that is fact, or opinion firmly based on experience. This chapter is different because it deals with what *might* happen. Some of this is easily predictable because it is an extrapolation of a trend, or in some cases is happening now in more forward-looking organisations. The rest is speculation. The various possibilities do not form a coherent vision of the future, indeed some may contradict each other. However, I hope it is useful to those interested in possible future developments as a source of ideas and as a spur to experimentation.

The chapter ends with a 'health warning' about the future.

New applications

Remuneration

There is little doubt that many organisations will move from using 360-degree feedback simply for development purposes towards making the data at least a part-determinant of pay.

The experience of PRC/Litton described in Chapter 13 gives some interesting insights into how to approach this issue. They did not do everything at once. Instead, they used the technique initially as a developmental tool and only moved to pay afterwards. This enabled employees to get used to the idea of multi-rater assessment and to have confidence in the concept before moving to more controversial applications.

It is quite a safe bet to predict that other organisations will try it. It does, however, raise the old issue of the dangers of linking pay to appraisal. There is a strong school of thought in favour of keeping appraisal primarily as a means of development and separating it from pay issues. The argument is that if appraisal is used for remuneration purposes the latter will become dominant in people's minds and development needs will receive less attention. A partial answer appears to be to have a gap between the feedback process and decisions on remuneration. Some companies are making this gap as long as 9 to 12 months.

The other issue which organisations will have to address is the undoubted fact that everybody regards remuneration as important. It is a hygiene factor which, when neglected or threatened, causes trouble. Knowing your development needs is one thing. Realising that next year's bonus will depend in part, for example, on how your team members rate your contribution to the team in terms of helpfulness and co-operative behaviour is another, hotter issue. The means of measurement will come under close scrutiny. Those responsible for it will need to be able to demonstrate that the instrument used measures accurately what it sets out to measure. Test developers and users will have to convince participants, their managers and other raters that the instrument, its administration and all other associated matters conform to best practice. Failure to do this will result either in direct conflict, or passive resistance in the form of non-responses, ones which are so middle-of-the-road as to be useless, or unspoken collusion of the 'I'll scratch your back if you scratch mine' kind.

Strategic analysis

Another interesting application which is not yet common is the use of the data for strategic purposes. It seems that organisations have not yet realised how useful such data can be in studying the needs and strengths of a given group of people. In Chapter 3 we saw that Ashridge Management College use 360-degree feedback on a senior management programme they have run in recent years. Participants on this programme are a cross-section of managers from a variety of public and private-sector organisations. Some 200 people have been through it. This means that data is available from over 1,500 respondents, of which about 700 are direct reports. Taking an aggregate view of the scores given by reports reveals some very interesting findings.

The instrument measures importance at the competency level and current versus expected performance at the item level. The higher the importance rating (out of nine) the more the importance. The greater the average gap size the lower the performance in the competency in question. An examination of the importance ratings in Table 23 shows that skill areas like personal integrity, communicating and empowerment are seen as much more important by employees than their managers' technical competencies. It is interesting that they do not attach much importance to creativity and innovation either. Yet the skill effectiveness ranking in Table 24 shows that technical competence is the managers' main strength (relative to requirements rather than in absolute terms). Comparing the two sets of rankings shows little correlation between what these managers are good at and the important parts of the job.

Ashridge can put this kind of information to some use in making sure that their programmes match up with development needs. Yet, if all these people belonged to one organisation instead of several, think how useful this data would be to

Table 23

RANKING OF 16 LEADERSHIP COMPETENCIES BY IMPORTANCE

Importance Ratings LAS–Ashridge		
Ranking	**Competency**	**Average Rating by staff/support**
I	*Personal Integrity*	7.6
2	*Communicating*	7.4
3	*Empowerment*	7.2
4	**Initiative and risk-taking**	6.6
4	**Problem-solving**	6.6
4	*Delegating*	6.6
4	*Motivating*	6.6
4	*Teamwork*	6.6
9	**Quality of results**	6.4
9	*Vision*	6.4
I I	**Planning and goal-setting**	6.2
12	*Mentoring*	6.0
13	*Coaching*	5.8
14	*Diversity*	5.6
15	**Creativity and innovation**	5.4
16	**Technical competencies**	4.8
Task-oriented competencies/*Person-oriented competencies*		

Table 24

RANKING OF 16 LEADERSHIP COMPETENCIES BY EFFECTIVENESS

Overview – Skill Effectiveness – LAS – Ashridge		
Ranking	**Competency**	**Average Gap by staff/support**
1	**Technical competencies**	0.51
2	**Quality of results**	0.53
3	**Initiative and risk-taking**	0.58
4	**Problem-solving**	0.60
5	*Personal integrity*	0.63
6	**Creativity and innovation**	0.64
7	*Empowerment*	0.68
8	*Communication*	0.70
9	*Motivating*	0.72
10	*Teamwork*	0.76
11	*Vision*	0.79
12	*Mentoring*	0.80
13	*Diversity*	0.83
14	*Delegating*	0.85
15	**Planning and goal-setting**	0.90
15	*Coaching*	0.90
Task-oriented competencies/*Person-oriented competencies*		

senior management. The conclusion I have reached from this analysis is that people seem to be promoted for what they are good at now, rather than for what is important in the new job. In other words, as technical competence is of questionable value in the higher job should we not be looking for other skills and abilities in potential promotees? Why are our recruitment, development and career planning systems producing these patterns? What do we need to change so that we have senior managers with more appropriate strengths?

Another way of analysing these results is to divide the list between people-oriented competencies (shown in italics) and task-centred competencies (show in bold). In the importance ranking there is no pattern, but the skill effectiveness ranking clearly shows many more strengths in the task areas, and most of the development needs in the people-management field.

If this group was tested again then it would be possible to see not only whether there had been an improvement, but also how the strategic pattern of management strengths and weaknesses was moving over time. This is very useful data for longer-term planning.

As the amount of 360-degree feedback data available to an organisation grows, and as people learn how to use it, then the value of strategic analysis will be more properly recognised. Some human resources professionals might say 'We knew this all the time'. That may be so, but the knowledge is likely to be based on anecdotal evidence. If we are seeking to persuade top management to make expensive, far-reaching and courageous decisions on human resources issues, which is the better basis for persuading them – comprehensive hard data, or hunches?

Creating open cultures

In theory, as organisation cultures become more open, 360-degree feedback will not be needed. People will be much more willing to give and receive feedback openly and honestly. The theory says that there will be no need for questionnaires, sophisticated software, or elaborate reports. This scenario is possible, but is very unlikely to happen in practice. Organisations that want to change their culture usually include honest and straightforward dealings and open communications among their list of desirable values. However, it may be that only limited progress can be made in this area because of social trends which run counter to it. Some would say that modern society is less tolerant, trusting and open than it used to be, and that people put responsibility to themselves above that towards others. It is unlikely that 360-degree feedback would become unnecessary. It is unlikely that practitioners will work themselves out of a job. There will always be circumstances where confidential and anonymous feedback are valuable.

We shall probably find the technique being used increasingly as a vehicle of culture change, and adapting itself to take new forms. The majority of organisations have cultures that rely on, and support, anonymity protection and confidentiality as part of a performance feedback process. Many have approached the concept and practice of openness quite warily. Openness in this context can be defined as having the ability and comfort level to share performance feedback with others in an honest fashion. Most people in the workforce have not yet developed this type of comfort level. Who can blame them? Much of this is because in the past there has been no mechanism for developing it.

Organisations are now learning that the 360-degree feedback process is significantly opening up dialogue between work colleagues. Managers and employees alike assert that there is much more discussion between them regarding performance feedback. Employees are learning that their co-workers have needs and perceptions of which they were never aware until 360-degree feedback was implemented. For example, as employees interpret their feedback results, they find themselves faced with questions like 'Where do I go from here?' and 'Who else can I talk with to assist me with ideas for development and changing my behaviour?' Co-workers begin to see the value of honest face-to-face feedback once the door is opened. The continuation of these interactive discussions will increase comfort levels with openness.

As self-directed work teams gradually become the norm for many organisations, the need for frequent and direct feedback will become a big priority. Such teams will be required to produce and complete projects with increased speed and quality. Ultimately, team members will have no choice but to share performance feedback, face-to-face as a group, on a daily basis to ensure that all members are contributing equally and without error. To ask people to do this from a standing start is to ask a lot. However, 360-degree feedback can be used as a means of introducing such open behaviour more gently.

In the next millennium it is possible that organisations will move to other types of feedback processes that incorporate measures of both results and competence seen from multiple perspectives, but in a more direct fashion. For example, it is possible as technology in the workplace advances that 360-degree users will respond to specific questions or scenarios and send them back on-line to the person requesting the feedback. Follow up face-to-face discussion would still be an integral component of the feedback process. However, it would be greatly enhanced and streamlined by direct and candid responses to the participant.

Another possible future variation is that the performance feedback process will no longer depend on a once-a-year implementation. Employees would have the freedom and capability to ask for feedback at any time. This might be done by people who want to know how others see them to be progressing with a performance improvement plan. After all, why wait for twelve months to know whether or not others think you have developed? Again, this may be done on-line, face-to-face or by a combination of both methods.

The cultural possibilities mentioned above suggest that, for some, there will be less reliance on standard questionnaires with large numbers of rated questions. It is more likely that the information sought will be presented in qualitative form by means of more open-ended questions. This has implications on questionnaire design, probably promoting a more informal and less structured style of seeking feedback. Advances in automatic voice and handwriting recognition would assist this development.

Do-it-yourself

In recent years the competency movement has resulted in many organisations doing more work in-house. It has also seen a large amount of work done by outside specialists. I think it is likely that both phenomena will continue to appear in the 360-degree feedback field, but with some differences.

I hold no brief for the outside specialists. If I did it would be extremely odd behaviour to write a book for general circulation which went into great detail on how to design questionnaires, how to validate them, how to choose software, and how to facilitate feedback!

Some organisations will undoubtedly decide that they want to become self-sufficient in most stages of the 360-degree feedback process. Some will take a different route. Those who turn out to be happy with their choice of direction – whatever it is – will have taken informed decisions based on internal expertise, cost, time and confidentiality. They will also have considered whether the culture will support their choice. Let us take the stages of the process and examine them in the light of these issues. Many of the points have been discussed in earlier parts of the book, so this section concentrates on bringing them together, rather than re-analysing them.

Questionnaire design

If the expertise to design these specialised instruments, with its need for the use of quite specific language and understanding of behaviour, exists in the organisation, then it makes sense to use it. The costs may be lower than using an outsider. Time can be a problem because other duties might intervene to cause delays. Confidentiality is not an issue at this stage.

Validation

This is a stage whose importance many in-house professionals seem to have trouble in appreciating. Time and cost implications make it very tempting to cut corners, particularly when one questionnaire is an adaptation of something similar, and therefore appears to be valid. People forget that what was fine for one situation is inappropriate for another, or that adding or subtracting questions can change the effectiveness with which a questionnaire does its job.

There is much to be said for contracting out this stage to someone who has more dedicated resources, and who may be more objective. The wise gardener gets someone else to prune their roses! Many consultants themselves use other firms or academic institutions to help in the validation of their work. Independent validation can also help as a means of reassuring others that the instrument has received objective scrutiny.

Data collection and processing

This is probably the area where the issues are hardest to analyse. In Chapter 6 I described the costs and pricing of in-house processing systems and the resources needed to run and administer them. Bureau service processing can be more expensive, but when the comparisons are made, not necessarily by much. The real issue is probably how much freedom does an organisation want to customise its own questionnaires, running different ones in various divisions or locations?

Confidentiality of data collection and processing have also been covered elsewhere. Some will feel that they can never do these in-house. Some will gradually move towards them.

Others are capable now, based on their existing experience of the process.

Another issue to consider is that of the internally designed IT solution. In the early days of 360-degree feedback the user could sometimes get by using manual data entry and spread-sheets or other non-360-degree specific processing methods. This would be particularly so where numbers were small. However, the output is limited because it was based on software designed with general business presentation in mind, rather than the peculiar demands of 360-degree feedback. Most organisations are realising that the way forward from this is not more sophisticated solutions designed internally, but to go outside either to buy a ready-made system, or to use a bureau service. User needs change over time; so do developments in technology. Suppliers are constantly enhancing their products in line with these developments, something that the internal IT provider cannot do so readily.

Facilitation

The arguments against in-house facilitation revolve around resources, confidentiality, and to some extent status. As we discussed earlier, large numbers of participants require a substantial facilitator resource. Many internal people seem to accomplish the role well, given the proper training and support. Human resources functions are realising the value of having their own staff and other employees equipped with these skills. We are therefore likely to see a growth in the amount of facilitation conducted by internal people. This growth, however, could come to an abrupt end should there be any high profile accidents or failures caused by the over-enthusiastic use of poorly trained or wrongly accredited facilitators.

To conclude this debate it is worth considering what the future role or roles of the outside expert can be. The first is to carry out as many or as few of the main project stages as the client chooses to request. This will vary from all stages, to some, to none. Many clients who are at an early stage of experience or knowledge of 360-degree feedback overestimate their ability to carry it out. The more specialised a task is, for example statistical validation, facilitator training or supplying and installing software, the more likely it is that external help will be needed and sought. The larger an organisation is, the more it will want to use its internal resources, if it already possesses them.

The second role which may develop is as a consultant rather than a doer. This means someone who is trusted to inspect or evaluate what exists or what has been produced so far, who can solve problems, use experience from other organisations, and who can teach.

Integration with other systems

So far, 360-degree feedback has been used mainly in individual applications. The data collected is used for a single purpose, be that self-development, part of a training programme, performance appraisal and so on. Another future development is likely to be the multi-purpose use of this information. In this scenario it would become part of an all-round performance management system. Data from 360-degree feedback would be used for the development side of appraisal, extending into self-development plans, formal training, assessment or development centres, and finally remuneration. The purposes would be different, but linked. The data would be the same but would play a different part in each process. This may extend into career planning and selection. Just as traditional appraisal documentation can be used as part of the process of deciding whether a person is suitable for a vacancy, 360-degree feedback data can also be used. Databases can be set up containing performance data as well as other information about the individual, such as experience and qualifications. Job profiles can be constructed from competency frameworks and a search can be made for people within the organisation whose strengths match those required.

These developments have big implications for data storage and information management. Systems will appear that are capable of managing all these various uses either in combination or separately. Some advances are discussed in the section on technology.

Implementation across the organisation

In its development so far, 360-degree feedback has tended to concentrate first on senior management and has then spread downwards, if not very far, through the organisation. There are, however, many other people in and outside the organisation presently excluded who would benefit from it. Leaving considerations of cost and logistics aside, the main qualification to receive this type of feedback is to have a working relationship with others. Such a definition widens the net considerably. It applies to the car-park attendant as well as to the chief executive. However, there are still limits. Can it really be applied to the shop floor? The answer is yes, provided that people depend on and interact with each other in some way. I mentioned self-directed work teams earlier, because in these everyone is a stakeholder in their colleagues' performance and they interact sufficiently to observe each other's. Arguably then, improvements could appear if 360-degree feedback was put in place.

Some organisations have tackled the cost issues by simplifying the whole process. In other words, the questionnaires are very short and the feedback report is simple. Unfortunately the trade off between cost and usefulness is never satisfactory. Cheap, simple feedback for all might mean useful feedback for nobody.

Perhaps a better way to implement 360-degree feedback would be to do it gradually and selectively throughout the organisation, looking for the biggest pay-off from certain groups, whether managerial or not. Service providers are an example. Internal providers might be secretaries, human resources professionals, systems analysts, maintenance engineers and facilities staff. External providers might be sales people, customer services staff, car break-down patrols, or police constables. All these jobholders would qualify. The way to do it cheaply as well as effectively is to concentrate on specific competencies which the organisation wants to emphasise, either generally or in certain jobs, before moving on to others.

As organisations move from real to virtual scenarios people's relationships with each other change. Yes, you still communicate, but there are subtle differences. 360-degree feedback could help people improve their communication skills in situations where there is only remote yet vital contact in the relationship. Examples might be people who use the Internet or intranets to communicate.

Other examples are groups that are part of the organisation, yet not part of it. Temporary staff, contractors, consultants and other suppliers can be seen as sources of feedback. You can also regard them as associate members of the organisation who have a right to receive 360-degree feedback.

Let me finally mention another group, many of whom are not only unused to multi-rather feedback, but who also may rarely have received any feedback. This consists of the professions – doctors, lawyers, accountants, teachers. As the culture changes in these professions their members too will find themselves giving and receiving the new form of performance feedback.

Technology

Technology is a major driver of change within the 360-degree feedback assessment industry. There is not space here to cover every facet. Chapter 6 touches on some of the advances in data collection, including on-line solutions. One novel form of data collection of which we may see more is IVR, or interactive voice response. The PRC/Litton case study in Chapter 13 provides an interesting example of this. The technology is with us now, waiting for more organisations to adopt it.

In this short section I will look at data processing technology and how it may develop. If we were to categorise current and future 360-degree feedback technology we might identify three levels:

Level 1 – Diagnostic

This represents the majority of current systems. They allow users to define and perform assessments that are customised to the specific organisation's needs. They also provide a large number of reporting capabilities that help to diagnose performance problems at individual or organisation-wide levels.

Level 2 – Prescriptive

This level of sophistication begins to introduce some basic artificial intelligence that links knowledge about interventions (ie how to improve a given behaviour) to the results of an assessment. There are few existing systems claiming to provide this capability. In addition, the current sophistication of artificial intelligence is quite shallow. It permits only a rather mechanistic approach, making the solutions of questionable value. In addition, most of the current systems are tied to a standard instrument, limiting their perceived relevance to the diverse needs of organisations.

Level 3 – Active

This level of technology would use artificial intelligence actively to assist in the management of human resources through a monitoring process. It would provide support for the management of employees, for example by recommending the membership of teams for projects, deducing and pointing to organisational weaknesses, and fitting people to jobs that meet their capabilities and aspirations. Also at this level would be the capability for technology to access other linked human resources with IT systems, providing secure yet accessible multi-purpose uses of 360-degree feedback data mentioned earlier in this chapter.

A final and most interesting technological development will be the use of the Internet or intranets for 360-degree feedback. Some organisations are starting to use local or wide area networks for this purpose, but there may be more to come. In future years we may see development activities de-coupled from corporate influence, with people accessing 360-degree feedback questionnaires on the Internet and receiving their feedback from the same medium, linked to specific development solutions.

Health warning

Here I offer a list of 'dos' and 'don'ts' that could make 360-degree feedback a powerful, effective and permanent component of human resources management, seen as indispensable by those who use it. By implication I also offer some views on what could confine the technique to marginal use, cause it to be seen with mistrust and suspicion, or indeed consign it to the history of techniques which started with promise and ended in oblivion.

DO seek out what is best practice and follow it, even if this is not always convenient.

DON'T be tempted to cut corners for the sake of expediency, or confuse best practice with current practice.

DO see 360-degree feedback as a system with many parts needing equal attention.

DON'T concentrate on the easier or more interesting parts at the expense of briefing, facilitation, and post-assessment support.

DO see it as a measurement tool which can have many applications if used appropriately.

DON'T view it as an end in itself or as a panacea.

DO keep your promises on confidentiality and anonymity.

DON'T allow these to be compromised by people or systems.

DO keep your promises on what the technique will be used for.

DON'T use it for purposes for which it was not advertised or intended.

DO introduce it into the organisation in a planned and, if necessary, gradual way.

DON'T try to do things too quickly.

DO expect that it will cause ripples in the organisation, both before and after implementation.

DON'T assume that it will be universally welcomed.

DO use it regularly.

DON'T see it as a one-off exercise.

Part IV

360-DEGREE
FEEDBACK IN PRACTICE

10

THE AUTOMOBILE ASSOCIATION

Using 360-degree feedback to stimulate and measure culture change

The Automobile Association (AA) is a household name in the UK. It has positioned itself as an integral part of life in Britain. Corporate advertising such as its 'fourth emergency service' campaign is intended to strengthen this image. Whenever issues on motoring arise on radio or television, from weather and traffic conditions to the interests of the ordinary motorist, there is usually an interview with a representative of the AA.

This is a far cry from 1905, when the AA was founded to protect the interests of beleaguered pioneer motorists. The organisation has grown from a modest lobby with £100 in the bank to a huge and diversified business group with over nine million members, 3.5 million customers, more than 12,000 staff and 40 different business activities.

In addition to the traditional roadside breakdown service, the AA has many other functions. These include vehicle inspections, a wide range of insurance including health, home, life and personal accident, as well as car insurance, financial services, retailing, countless publications from cartography to hotel services, AA roadwatch, and driving instruction.

In 1989 the organisation was decentralised into business units: Membership, Insurance, Financial Services, Retail and Commercial Services with an influential Corporate Group. Headquartered in Basingstoke, it has offices, shops, and service centres throughout the UK and continental Europe.

The management population consists of some 700 people in five levels, from the director general downwards. The human resources function is well established. The group personnel director has a small central staff, with most of the function devolved to the divisions.

For many years the AA has been an enthusiastic researcher into what its members and customers think of the services provided. In 1993 the AA turned its market research inwards by means of an employee opinion survey called Pulse. This is now run on a 12-monthly basis. It seeks to gain employee views on matters such as how well the organisation cares for their well-being, communicates with them, and provides opportunities for personal growth and development. There are also questions that deal with specific aspects of their job, such as workload, pay, treatment, and their boss. Results show the AA's position on an index known as the 'transitional norm for organisations undergoing major change'. It is therefore able to measure its position and progress against those of other organisations in a similar situation. The survey was begun partly because of the realisation that the standards of service provided by customer-facing staff in service organisations depend very much on the prevailing standards of management. Thus, an employee who is well-led, informed, motivated and trained is more likely to provide good customer service than someone who does not benefit from such effective management.

In 1995 it became apparent that there was a continuing disparity between the perceptions of those inside the organisation and those outside it. The 'Pulse' results on employee opinions showed that management practices needed to be changed to keep up with the needs and aspirations of a developing workforce. The AA needed to take action immediately on this, because it realised that the *status quo*, if left unchanged, would eventually work its way out of the organisation and into the minds of the public. The medium for this would be the performance and attitudes of employees, particularly those whose job involved customer contact.

In 1995 the AA developed a detailed, research-based document to describe the standards of management behaviour that the organisation wished to value and promote. Entitled 'Management standards we can trust' and reflecting the words of its mission statement as shown in Table 25, it sets out the values and behaviours that the organisation expects its man-

Table 25

AA MISSION STATEMENT

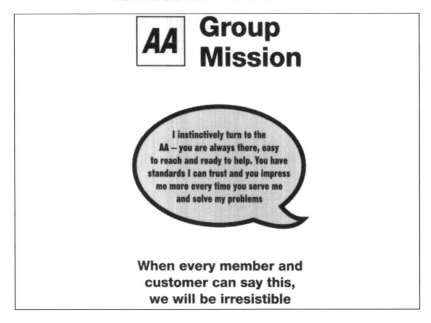

When every member and customer can say this, we will be irresistible

agers to demonstrate in their everyday dealings with employees. The AA took a decision to use 360-degree feedback as one of the prime levers of change. It planned to assess all 700 managers over a period of time. The assessment would result in development plans, built into the AA's management development system, and consequent behavioural change. It also intended to provide considerable support to all managers in their attempts to change. Performance would be remeasured after an interval of two years.

Questionnaire design

The organisation took great pains to ensure that the 360-degree feedback questionnaire focused only on those competencies that belonged to the manager's management of their staff to achieve effective performance. The designers drew the initial list of categories and definitions from the management standards document itself, and other internally-used competency descriptions. It included categories such as example-setting, demonstrating high personal standards, expecting high standards from others, encouraging openness, earning and showing trust, delegating, giving clear direction, communicating, and showing concern. It deliberately excluded other categories as not being in the 'people-centred' area. These were such competencies as thinking skills, technical expertise, energy and drive, proactivity and decision-making.

This separation of two types of competency was the subject of considerable debate within the organisation. However, the prevailing view was that this was a highly focused project that should target only certain well-defined behaviours.

The original version of the management standards questionnaire (MSQ) contained 74 items. These were sent to 12 representatives of senior and middle management to scrutinise in terms of:

☐ the quality of the behavioural statements (appropriateness, clarity, repetition)
☐ the quality of the questionnaire (layout, ease of use, rating scale, etc)
☐ the process itself
☐ any issues about implementation.

The AA organised a meeting of this group so that views could be gathered and debated. This resulted in a reduction of the original version to 60 questions by eliminating repetitive items and refining the remainder.

The designers then repeated the process on another group, predominantly of human resources managers, resulting in further refinement and a reduction to 48 questions. The remaining questions were grouped under these categories:

☐ setting a leadership example
☐ building working relationships
☐ managing for results
☐ caring for people.

A six-point frequency scale was developed.

Piloting

The first pilot consisted of a group of 17 managers. Respondents were self, boss, direct reports, and peers/second level reports. In addition to the MSQ, all respondents received a validation questionnaire. They commented on the clarity and relevance of the questions and the scale.

The second pilot was for a group of eight managers with only self, boss, and direct reports as respondents. It included a six-point effectiveness scale.

A team of four external and two internal experts carried out one-to-one facilitation with all members of both groups. The views of these people, the feedback from participants and respondents, and various other validation measures and analyses, helped the design team to take informed decisions on the final format of the questionnaire and the feedback report.

As part of the piloting process participants received their reports at a series of group debriefing sessions. One issue raised was the problem of not being able to guarantee anonymity of opened-ended responses, and that the instructions needed further clarification. These opinions, however, reinforced the view of open-ended questions as a very useful part of the feedback process. This was because they illustrated a lot of the messages coming from the graphical and numerical parts of the report. Other issues raised at these meetings included:

☐ instructions
☐ anonymity
☐ role of the boss
☐ report layout and content
☐ gender issues.

In the first pilot group peers had some difficulty in answering a number of the questions. This was because they were unable to observe management of people actually taking place. It led to a decision to use the MSQ for upwards feedback only, provided by direct and second-level reports. Peer input was not sought. Comments on the scale showed that respondents had difficulty in using it. Also, there was insufficient separation between participants' scores. An effectiveness scale was therefore developed.

Final questionnaire format

As a result of the pilots further revisions were made to the questionnaire. The final number of questions increased to 50;

the number of respondents was finalised at 10 (self, boss, direct reports and second level reports); the effectiveness scale remained.

It was decided to collect demographic data from the questionnaire. This consisted of business area, tier, and gender.

The next step was for the AA's top 50 managers to take part in the process, and to receive either internal or external one-to-one facilitation.

At the time of writing 350 managers have been through the process. Each participant receives 10 questionnaires and detailed instructions on how to choose and approach respondents. Completed questionnaires go back directly to an external processing organisation. In order to maximise people's trust in the confidentiality and anonymity of the process the AA is at pains to stress to its employees that no copies are kept, and that all completed questionnaires and the results database remain outside the organisation.

Facilitation

Facilitators receive the reports for their allotted participants, and set up a one- to two-hour feedback session. Further sessions may be organised. The participant is expected to share their feedback with their boss, in a manner of their own choosing. Participants are also advised how they can share and clarify their feedback with others in a sensitive way that respects confidentiality and anonymity. Anecdotal evidence has suggested that acceptance of the instrument was enhanced where the participant's boss had shared their own feedback and action plan.

There are now some 50 internal facilitators. Two-thirds of them are specially selected line managers, and the remainder are human resources specialists. The training and accreditation of facilitators are done using both internal and external expertise. Pre-training starts with their own feedback. Formal training lasts one or two days, depending on the level of the trainees. It consists of theory, discussion and role playing. The contents cover the design of the questionnaire, the finer points of report layout, including statistical and anonymity issues, preparing for the feedback session, and training in the principles and practices of feedback, as outlined in Chapter 6 of this book. Participants are required to demonstrate their skills in role play and are assessed by both internal and external experts. Most of those going through the training receive immediate accreditation, some do not and have further supervised practice. A small minority do not receive accreditation at all. All facilitators are carefully monitored, with feedback to a central point.

The intended ratio of facilitators to participants is 1:15. This means that, over a two-year period, each facilitator will have to carry out about 15 one-to-one sessions. This is the only mandatory requirement of them. However, they are encouraged to develop their role within the organisation as they see fit, by arranging follow-up sessions and by helping with feedback sharing. The next challenge for them will come shortly, when they are asked to revisit participants with a copy of the re-test. The facilitation of the messages from re-testing, be they positive, negative or the *status quo*, will require further briefing.

A big advantage of the AA's approach to the use of internal facilitators is that they have developed a substantial number of committed, skilled and influential people at several levels of the organisation who are expert in the concepts and practices of the new culture. This in itself will be a major factor in achieving change.

Development support

The AA commissioned a specially written self-development guide that all participants receive with their feedback report. Its purpose is to supplement (not replace) the live facilitation they receive. Each of the 50 rated questions is discussed, together with some ideas and tips on what the participant can do to improve their performance in this specific area.

The self-development guide also contains ideas on other approaches that the participant may take to develop themselves. These include:

☐ behaviour working groups, where people with similar needs get together as a mutual self-help group
☐ peer mentoring where the participant chooses someone at their own level from another department as a development adviser

☐ self-development coaching groups, specially-convened groups using a facilitator or expert coach to discuss specific performance issues

☐ one-off lectures by visiting experts

☐ sharing/clarifying sessions with boss or staff

☐ performance contracts in which the participant makes a formal contract with specified others that they will not behave in a certain way.

Learning resource centre

The AA has now set up a learning resource centre as a joint venture with a local college. It provides an environment where individuals can learn and develop at their own pace in a convenient, on-site setting. Its aim is to enhance structured, classroom training rather than replace it, catering for individuals' differing learning styles. It contains an extensive selection of programmes on CD-ROM or video aimed at improving knowledge, self-awareness and behaviour in the areas set out in the 'management standards we can trust' document.

Coaching support

During the course of the project, and indeed previously, anecdotal evidence has suggested that many middle managers lack enough coaching skills to have an impact on their staff's performance. This has been corroborated by a strategic analysis of the feedback data gathered so far. The organisation has therefore put in place a series of coaching workshops for many managers in this population. The training will serve two purposes: in addition to a generally beneficial effect, it will enable managers to respond more effectively as their own staff receive feedback and begin to require help in improving their performance.

Results

The AA plans to implement a large-scale, interim evaluation project using an approach similar to that illustrated in Appendix E. Ex-participants will be asked what they thought of the quality and value of their feedback, the extent to which their own manager has been involved, their views on confidentiality, and what impact the whole process has had on them. Ex-respondents (who are also direct or second level reports) will be asked what changes they have noticed in their manager's behaviour, and what they think about being part of the process.

Retesting itself will commence in 1998, so no statistical data will be available until then. However, anecdotal evidence suggests that individuals are responding positively and changing the way that they manage.

Peter Stemp, group personnel director, says:

The upwards feedback process is providing a very effective catalyst for individual improvement and development amongst managers at all levels. Anecdotal and survey data on the way that AA people are now managed is providing evidence of fundamental cultural change. I am sure that we could not have achieved as much without the controlled power of upwards appraisal.

11

ARCO

Using 360-degree feedback to build teamwork

This chapter describes a case involving an innovative project using 360-degree feedback assessments in an organisation change programme aimed primarily at enhancing teamwork. This project, still underway, is being conducted in a merchant fleet of petroleum tankers. Kenneth Brousseau of Decision Dynamics Group and Michael Perrault of Advanced Teamware, Inc, who are leading the 360-degree feedback portion of this on-going effort, provided the findings and data reported here.

Atlantic Richfield Company, known as ARCO, is a major oil producer and petroleum products distributor in the USA. ARCO, headquartered in Los Angeles, California, is one of the prime developers of the crude oil fields in Alaska. Alaskan crude is gathered from the northern slopes of the state and transported via pipeline to the port of Valdez in the southern section of the state. The oil is then shipped via sea-going vessels, primarily to the west coast of the USA.

ARCO Marine Incorporated (AMI), a US registered flag carrier, operates ten steam ships in its fleet. Eight of the ships are crude oil tankers plying the waters of the eastern Pacific Ocean transporting cargo from Valdez to ports in Seattle, Washington, San Francisco, and Long Beach, California. The remaining two ships are known as 'product ships', and transport petroleum products such as jet fuel, benzene and kerosene. These product ships operate in the Gulf of Mexico, transit the Panama Canal and also serve the US west coast.

AMI employs approximately 900 people, 600 of whom actually travel at sea. The remainder of the people provide on-shore support to the fleet. These services include voyage scheduling, supply requisition, personnel staffing, engineering, health, safety and environmental engineering. The 600 people assigned to the fleet are further divided into two major

categories: licensed and unlicensed seamen, based upon qualification by the United States Coast Guard. Licensed merchant
mariners are qualified to operate vessels as either deck officers
or engine officers.

ARCO ships are organised into three departments: the deck
department, the engine department and the steward department.
The deck department operates the vessel, loads and unloads
cargo, and in general maintains all parts of the vessel outside of
the engine room. The engine department, as one would guess, is
responsible for the propulsion of the ship, its electric power generation, water purification and the on-board cargo pumping system. The steward department prepares and serves meals to the
crew and provides minimal housekeeping support.

Within the deck department's licensed officers one finds the
ship's captain, the first mate, second mate and third mate.
These officers are responsible for the operation and navigation
of the vessel, and while at sea one of them is on duty on the
ship's bridge at all times. The engine department's licensed
officers are the chief engineer, the 1st assistant, 2nd assistant
and 3rd assistant engineers. These officers man the engine
room twenty-four hours a day. Able-bodied seamen, unlicensed
deck hands, support the deck officers while unlicensed, but
highly specialised engine men assist the engine officers. A
senior unlicensed deck hand is assigned as the boatswain and
oversees the able-bodied seamen in the daily conduct of their
work. A pumpman is assigned to operate the vast array of tub-
ing, piping and pumps that onloads and offloads the dangerous
cargo.

The steward's department consists of three people; the chief
steward, a cook-baker and a mess person.

The American Merchant Marine is steeped in tradition. A
ship's captain is, to this day, titled as the Ship's Master. The
implications of the title are broad indeed, and convey the sense
of hierarchy one finds on board a merchant marine vessel. This
paramilitary organisation benefits from the swift carrying out
of orders typically found in disciplined organisations. Simultaneously, it also suffers from many of the disadvantages of a
rigorous, structured environment.

In March, 1989 the American shipping industry was rocked
to its foundation when the Exxon Valdez ran aground in the

pristine waters of Prince William Sound, the waterway leading to the port of Valdez. Its ruptured hull spilled millions of gallons of crude oil into the sound, fouling the environment. It was the single worst marine environmental disaster in the history of the USA. The effects of the spill are being contested in the courts.

Reports analysing the grounding of the Exxon Valdez indicate that the accident did not result from the failure of any piece of equipment. Rather, the analyses highlight breakdowns in human interaction as the primary causes. In particular, crew members failed to clarify their communication with each other and failed to explain or question several significant deviations from normal operating procedures prior to the grounding. Instead, the crew continued to behave in a structured and routine way in a very non-routine situation.

AMI and the entire ARCO organisation recognised that such an incident involving an ARCO ship would put the company out of business. ARCO simply does not have the capital to absorb such a loss. Jerry Aspland, then president of ARCO Marine, firmly believed that the rigid hierarchical culture found aboard merchant vessels was a major contributor to the risk of accidents, large and small. In fact, analysis of past incidents aboard ARCO vessels indicated that reluctance among crew members to point out possible errors to captains and other officers had played an important role in setting the stage for accidents. Accordingly, Aspland set about changing the culture in the ARCO fleet with particular emphasis on boosting levels of teamwork, co-operation, and collaboration among shipmates.

AMI embarked upon a multi-year process to shift shipboard working relationships among the officers and crew. The first step involved educating the masters and chief engineers regarding their decision-making styles. This process gave the participants a greater understanding and appreciation of how they and others think, process information and make decisions – a critical element in crisis situations. This preliminary intervention was followed by a series of conferences where the masters and chiefs were asked to provide input regarding the management of the fleet, and were introduced to team development concepts. Additionally, the masters and chiefs were involved in a series of physically challenging, outdoor team-development activities. Levels of trust increased as the participants learned first-hand, in a safe environment, the profound impact of collaboration and teamwork.

The next step in the strategy was to put intact ship's crews through team training initiatives. This involved crews who normally work with each other, but who at the time were on their rotational time off. This gave the shipmates an opportunity to learn more about each other and to develop collaborative problem-solving techniques. Within another year, those people who man the ship's bridge were put through a formal and highly technical training process called bridge team management training. This training involves the use of mechanical simulators and a series of crises that truly test and measure a team's response to the rigours and demands of managing a large vessel.

The AMI culture change strategy contained another critical component. While all previous training and education efforts were aimed at improving collaboration, teamwork and, ultimately, a ship's efficiency, ARCO needed a way to gauge the progress of each individual's efforts at becoming a 'team player'. To help them assess headway in this key area, AMI engaged Decision Dynamics Group (DDG), a consultancy in southern California. DDG, who had been working with the fleet for a number of years, employed a product named TeamView/360 to measure individual and team effectiveness. The DDG consultants travelled with the ships and conducted the assessments at sea, in the working environment.

TeamView/360, a Windows-based software product, is designed to be used with intact work groups. That is, groups or teams where an above-average level of interdependency exists between team-mates. An ideal setting is one where team members have frequent interaction; enough so that they develop perceptions of each other's effectiveness. Perceptions, for better or worse, significantly impact people's behaviour towards each other; in other words, *perception becomes reality*.

The TeamView/360 model requires participants to evaluate their own effectiveness for 31 specific, team-related behaviours. Following their self-evaluation, the participants then evaluate the effectiveness of each of their team-mates for the same 31 behaviours. The evaluations are considered to be 360-

degree feedback because they are coming from team members all around the individual. The questionnaires are completed manually and collected by the consultants to maintain privacy and confidentiality of the ratings.

The consultant enters the data from the questionnaires into the software program (installed on laptop computers) and a series of graphs and reports are generated automatically for each participant. Scores are compared against a normative database so people can see how they view their own performance against a standard for self-ratings. The ratings of their performance by their team-mates are similarly compared against a standard for other ratings. The software also computes a team average by compiling all the self-ratings and, separately, other ratings to generate a team profile.

The results are immediate and compelling. Within twenty-four hours of completing the questionnaires, participants are able to see graphically how they rate themselves compared to how their team-mates evaluate their effectiveness as a team player. Similarly, they learn where they stand in the team. They can compare the ratings they received from their team-mates with the average for the team. In other words, they learn where they are seen as outperforming the team and where they are negatively impacting the team.

The consultants schedule a one-hour, one-to-one interview with each participant to review their scores. This is followed, approximately two days later, by a team meeting during which the participants are encouraged to exchange feedback and perceptions about each other's behaviours, facilitated by the consultants. This meeting is absolutely critical to the success of the effort. The feedback exchange develops trust, openness and candour among shipmates, and provides dramatic proof of a shift in the culture of the organisation.

A review of the TeamView/360 data from the fleet reveals many interesting findings. Some 200 officers (licensed personnel) have participated in the TeamView/360 process. Of this number, 18 (roughly 10 per cent of the population) have been evaluated on two separate occasions. This occurs because the officers are on 60-day rotational assignments. They serve at sea for 60 days and then go off duty for 60 days, after which they return to sea. Therefore, as the consultants travelled from ship to ship, they occasionally encountered an officer who had been through the TeamView/360 process on another ship or, on the same ship, but with a different crew.

We shall focus on those participants for whom we have two sets of TeamView/360 data. Reviewing the scores of these individuals, we find dramatic differences between the first and second evaluations. Learning how others view their performance during the first assessment helped them focus on changing their inappropriate behaviours and thus, change the perceptions that others held of them. We see marked improvement in their TeamView/360 scores from the first assessment to the second assessment. Virtually all of the 18 people reflect an improvement in scores. Of particular significance is the fact that several of these people were on different ships with different crews while others were on the same ship with somewhat different crews. In both cases, we see elevated scores during the second assessment.

Figure 22 shows TeamView/360 scores for the chief engineer, reflecting his results for the first assessment. You will note that he fared quite well in the factors on the left side of the graph. These are the left-brain, technical, task-oriented behaviours. His highest-rated factor, controlling, is the epitome of the task-oriented behaviours and it is here that he scores highest.

However, on the social and interpersonal behaviours (the right-brain behaviours, displayed on the right side of the graph), this chief did not score so well. In fact, his scores are below average. These graphs gave him specific information that was later confirmed during the team feedback exchange meeting. This chief learned that he was seen as rigid, domineering and over-controlling. He was described as a micro-manager, a 'nit-picker'.

Apparently the chief engineer took to heart what he read on his graphs and heard from his shipmates. Over the course of the following months he made a concerted effort to change how he related to others. During the team meeting they had asked him to impart his years of experience and wisdom to the younger, up-and-coming engineers. In the interim period he assumed a coaching role with the younger people. He taught, trained and developed all the people in the engine room. Instead of waiting for them to fail before he would offer

Figure 22

CHIEF ENGINEER – FIRST ASSESSMENT

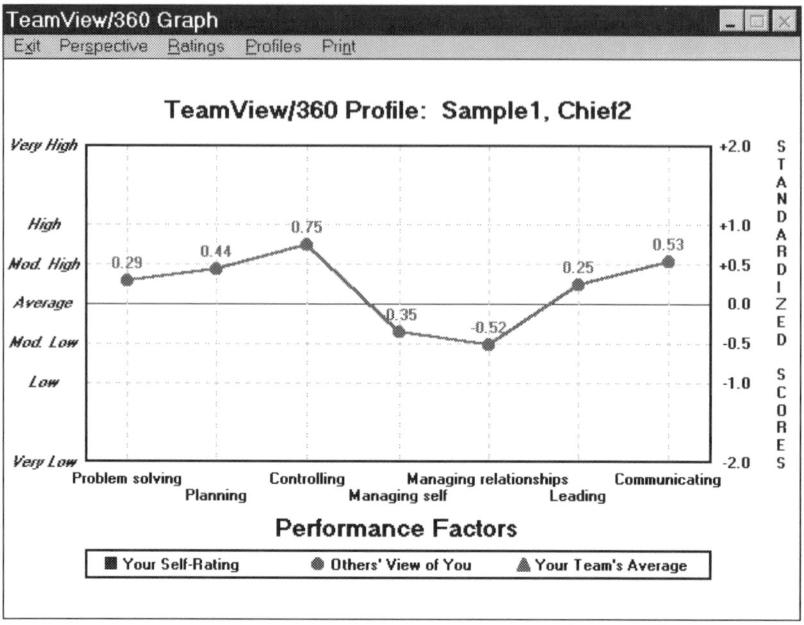

© Advanced Teamware

criticism and counsel, he now intervened earlier and showed them the correct procedure. Over the course of 10 months he changed his behaviours and they, in response, changed their views of him. Figure 23 shows his TeamView/360 scores from a slightly different crew, taken 10 months later. These dramatic differences truly show what can happen when a person heeds the feedback of team-mates and fulfils a commitment to change behaviours.

Particularly noteworthy are the results for the other people on whom data was collected from two assessments. Although the data sample is small, representing about 10 per cent of the population assessed, those with second evaluations show higher scores the second time around. We believe this clearly demonstrates the power of multi-rater feedback systems, such as TeamView/360.

The AMI TeamView/360 project is nearing completion of its first cycle. By combining all individual results we can also get

Figure 23

CHIEF ENGINEER – SECOND ASSESSMENT

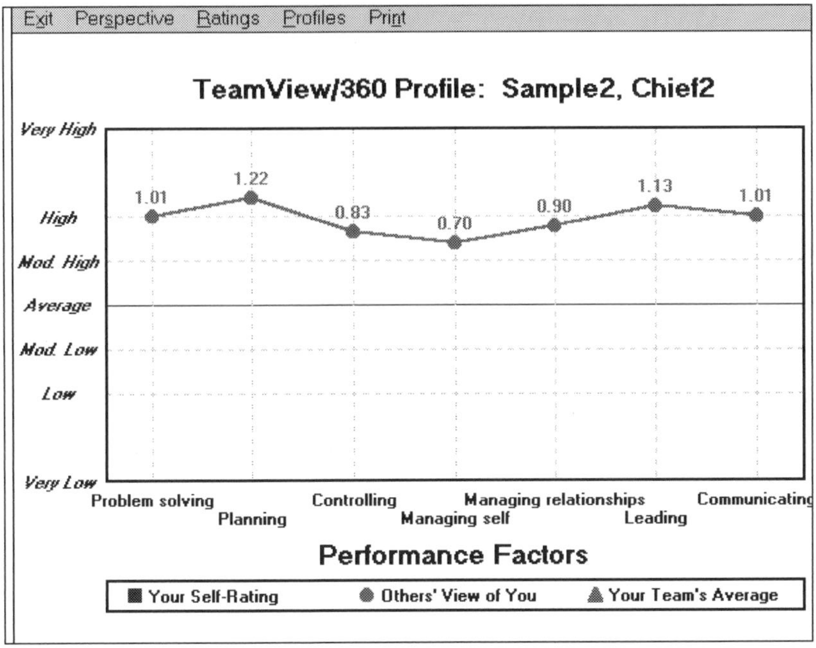

TeamView/360 Profile: Sample2, Chief2

© Advanced Teamware

a profile for the entire fleet. Observing those results, we learn that the officers tend to rate themselves lower than the average managers on whom we have collected data, and that they are rated higher than average by their shipmates. We believe that their lower self-ratings (we attribute this to a modest and unassuming self-concept) opens them to input from others and thus helps them to be seen more favourably by their shipmates. This measurement reflects the fact that the culture change effort which began five years earlier has taken root in the fleet.

Another indication of the persuasiveness of the culture change is that the unlicensed crew members, having seen the results obtained by the officers, have asked to participate in a similar project. This is particularly noteworthy because initially the TeamView/360 project was viewed with scepticism and mistrust throughout the fleet.

12

TOTAL OIL MARINE PLC

Using 360-degree feedback as a measure of values and as part of career development

The Total Group is a major international oil and gas company operating in 80 countries throughout the world. Its businesses span all the activities involved in bringing oil and natural gas to the consumer. These include both upstream exploration, development and production of oil and gas, and the down-stream refining and marketing of petroleum products, as well as the trading and transportation of crude oil and finished products. Exploration and production operations are concentrated in the Middle East, the Far East, Latin America, and the North Sea.

Total Oil Marine carries out Total's upstream operations in the UK and Ireland, with exploration taking place in the North Sea, west of Shetland, and in Irish waters. The company has been a major operator in the North Sea since oil was first discovered there and has established production operations at the Alwyn, Ellon and Dunbar fields. The gas terminal at St Fergus is a key link in the gas transportation system.

At the head office in Aberdeen and its various installations the company employs a skilled workforce with a large proportion of highly qualified scientists and engineers. The company has a significant number of French nationals on secondment, typically of two to four years. Long service is a feature of the UK workforce.

Senior management 360-degree feedback based on values and beliefs

In 1995, following a project to establish its values and beliefs as a company, Total Oil Marine commissioned a customised 360-degree feedback survey. The aim was to find out to what extent its senior management behaved in ways that were consistent with these values and beliefs. The starting point was the core values expressed in this list:

- results
- excellence
- professionalism
- teamwork
- learning partnerships
- recognition
- safety, health and the environment.

The Company carried out a lot of work to define further these headings. Thus 'excellence' consisted of:

- quality and continuous improvement
- the habits of a learning organisation
- vision, productivity and creativity
- striving for excellence in every technical discipline, function and business pursuit.

Each of the seven major headings and their sub-divisions then came under scrutiny to see what management competencies could be derived from them. This rested on the question: 'What main categories of behaviour will management need to carry out well in order to demonstrate that they are living the values and beliefs?' After many discussions with members of management this resulted in a list of 24 competencies, with associated definitions, covering such skill categories as:

Motivating The ability to create a satisfying work environment that encourages others to work towards achieving group goals.

Proactivity The ability to think ahead, influence events and take initiatives.

Assertiveness The ability to put forward an idea or an objection positively, calmly and incisively, without anger or embarrassment.

The company was satisfied at the end of this stage that it had produced a most exhaustive list of competencies. However, it saw a list of 24 as being unmanageable, particularly if this had then to be converted into behavioural statements measurable by a 360-degree feedback approach. The answer was to use importance ratings employed by some 360-degree feedback questionnaires as a means of prioritising competencies. Therefore, 24 members of top management received a questionnaire containing all 24 competencies, and were asked to rate each on a simple five-point importance scale from 'extremely important' to 'not important'. This resulted in a clear prioritisation of the 11 most important competencies:

☐ personal integrity
☐ decisions
☐ proactivity and forward thinking
☐ team leadership
☐ vision
☐ communicating
☐ quality of results
☐ business knowledge and sense
☐ empowerment
☐ motivating
☐ problem-solving.

The competency list then became the basis for the design of the questionnaire. The initial list had some 85 items, eventually reduced after discussion and revision to the final number of 51. One issue of potential difficulty was the impact of span of control. Where there were a large number of direct reports a special questionnaire was developed to rate at the competency level only.

Another issue that arose concerned individuals who might have to complete several questionnaires. Participants were asked to choose respondents (a maximum of 10) from four groups of self (mandatory) boss (mandatory) direct reports, peers and clients. The first participants came only from the top two levels of management, therefore there was a concern that some executives who had close working links with others across these groups would be targeted as respondents by too many people. The solution was to have the human resources function monitor who was being asked to respond, and manage any potential overloads, for example by suggesting that some participants change their choice of peer respondent. This intervention was seen as helpful, even though it meant that participants did not have a completely free hand over the choice of respondents.

A pilot was run, as a result of which minor revisions were implemented.

A particular feature of this project was the high degree of consultation and communication engaged in by the design team. In addition to consultation about competency definition and prioritisation, there was a group brief for the first 14 participants, who also represented the top management of the company. This covered:

☐ the purpose of the project
☐ introduction to the principles of 360-degree feedback
☐ how the questionnaire was designed and piloted
☐ how to choose and approach respondents
☐ anonymity and confidentiality
☐ administration
☐ timescales
☐ arrangements for feedback.

After questionnaire collection and external processing a group feedback session was run for the same group of 14 people. It consisted of:

☐ a recap of the project
☐ handing out the feedback reports
☐ explanation of the report format structure and detail
☐ advice on how to get clarification, how to share feedback and implement action plans
☐ arrangements for one-to-one facilitation.

Each report contained an individually-written commentary on the results.

Externally-conducted one-to-one facilitation sessions were then run for each member of this group, in order to assist with interpretation, learning, and action planning. These were seen as useful but the allocation of just one hour for each one meant that there was sometimes not enough time to explore the issues deeply enough. It left a feeling of slight dissatisfaction in some people, a lesson that the company has learned from, and applied in later projects.

Following the facilitation sessions the company commissioned an analysis of the composite results for the group as a whole, and parts of it. Data-reporting included analyses of:

☐ how people rated themselves compared to how others rated them (ie degree of self-knowledge)

☐ a composite ranking of all the competencies, thus showing areas of greatest improvement needs

☐ differences between line and staff, and other groups.

One interesting, but possibly predictable, finding was that the two different nationalities represented had markedly different performance profiles. The French nationals tended to be very strong in the intellectual competencies such as problem-solving and business knowledge and sense. The non-French, predominantly English and Scottish executives had strengths more in the people or relationship competencies, such as communicating and motivating.

General findings were that the company now had a much clearer view of what behaviours needed to change to underpin their values and beliefs, and how individuals needed to change to support this.

The project is still running, mainly using internal facilitators.

360-degree feedback for career and personal development

The second individual 360-degree feedback project that Total carried out was quite different from the first in several ways.

While the first project targeted only senior management (it has since started to be used at middle/senior management levels) the next was usable at any level within the organisation. Here is an extract from Total Oil Marine's 1995 Annual Report:

> The Company initiated a study on personal and career development in 1995. A multidisciplinary task force has recommended

the introduction of a personal development initiative encouraging staff to take responsibility for their own development while receiving quality support and encouragement from the Company. A new appraisal process known as '360-degree appraisal' has been applied to senior managers during 1995 and will become part of this initiative.

Whereas in the first project there was an expectation that all members of a defined group would take part, participation in the second was entirely voluntary, applied to employees in all parts and at all levels of the organisation, and was open to any employee who wanted to take part, regardless of whether they were 'fast track' people or not. While the first project had corporate ramifications (analyses of the needs of groups, for example) the second was solely for the individual. In the first project participants received direction and rules on the choice of respondent. In the second the only rule was: 'Does this person know you well enough to comment on your performance?'

The development feedback questionnaire (DFQ), as it came to be known, was part of a major attempt by Total to place personal or career development as much as possible into the hands of the participant, while at the same time providing support and encouragement. The personal development programme employs a three-level approach.

An extract from the staff communication document:

THE PERSONAL DEVELOPMENT PROGRAMME – A THREE-LEVEL APPROACH

This voluntary programme consists of three consecutive levels of involvement, explained below. You must start at level one before progressing to levels two and ultimately three.

It remains your decision whether or not to progress through the levels, and you are not required to gain entry to all levels in the one year, eg you may see it as appropriate to select level one and two in year one, and enter the full development programme in year two.

Programme level 1: Departmental review

☐ You discuss your development needs with your line supervisor and management, or senior person in your function.

☐ You agree personal development objectives.

☐ You progress this further through discussion with the human resources department.

☐ You complete your personal development plan.

Programme level 2: 360-degree development feedback

☐ You discuss your needs with the human resources department.

☐ You obtain 360-degree development feedback. This involves others that you select providing confidential feedback to you on your personal skills, aptitudes, strengths and weaknesses.

☐ You must use this information to confirm your development needs.

☐ You decide and obtain management approval to proceed to level three, if you so wish.

Programme level 3: Full development programme

☐ You attend a familiarisation workshop.

☐ You analyse your development options and needs in depth.

☐ You choose a mentor and learning support group.

☐ You implement the plan.

☐ You record, progress, review and adjust your plan over time.

As mentioned above, participation is entirely voluntary. The scheme has been advertised once and received over 100 expressions of interest, which are now being processed and actioned.

The design of the questionnaire posed particular problems because it was to be aimed at all organisational levels. This meant any management flavour had to be avoided, and the questions worded in everyday work language. The approach taken was to design a questionnaire in four parts, the first three of which were rated questions using a special six-point development scale.

Part 1 Personal skills. These are skills to do with basic personal competency or self-management.

Part 2 Skills with people. These included interpersonal skills such as listening, influencing, communicating, and teamworking.

Part 3 Technical competency. This included generic questions concerning the vocational skills within the job, and the extent to which the participant sought to develop them and also help other people to improve theirs.

Part 4 Career development. There is an innovative open-ended section that asks respondents to carry out a SWOT analysis on the participant's career prospects.

The result is a questionnaire that is applicable at all levels in the organisation. A particular feature concerns the choice of respondents. The selection carries no restrictions and participants are encouraged to be creative in their choice. Thus it is not uncommon to see friends and family members included. Respondents are not divided into groups, apart from the boss. Normally we would not recommend this, for the reasons outlined in Chapter 1, but here it is applicable because relationships with any particular group are not an issue here. The project is more concerned with how the participants appear to the outside world as represented by the respondents. It asks them to address how they should change in order to develop their career in a certain direction, rather than how they should change their dealings with particular groups. As with the first project, a textual commentary is prepared, and one-to-one facilitation is available.

Participants are enthusiastic about their feedback and show great commitment to the programme. The company is determined to support this as much as it can, and has made public its commitment:

> The company requires competent, motivated people at every level to achieve its business goals. All of us need to work to the maximum of our potential and be constantly searching for ways to develop and improve their performance ... I strongly recommend that you take advantage of these facilities and opportunities for personal development at the level you find appropriate.

> Lucien Lallier
> Managing Director
> Total Oil Marine PLC

13

PRC/LITTON INDUSTRIES

Integration of 360-degree feedback into human resource systems, including pay

This chapter describes a case which involves a hi-tech application of data collection combined with the linking of 360-degree feedback to pay and bonuses. This process, which has since become a part of the organisation's human resources performance management system, was conducted by Feedback Plus who assisted with initial instrument design, piloting, training and processing software installation.

PRC, a division of Litton Industries, and based in McLean, Virginia, is a leading supplier of information technology systems, products and services. The company has a variety of government and commercial customers. They have worked for the Department of Defense on implementing a large client/server-based contract, have redesigned the national weather forecasting system, and created document management systems for the Patent Office. They have maintained the data centre for the Executive Office of the President of the USA.

The company employs some 7,500 staff on 200 sites. The workforce is highly qualified, expecting to work in and enjoy a hi-tech environment.

In 1992 PRC's federal systems group had to restructure and downsize in order to meet the needs of the marketplace. The restructuring was extensive in scope. It also included the adoption of a quality-driven management approach, and a team-based structure, with all the organisational and cultural implications that such changes normally imply.

In order to make the re-structuring decisions needed, PRC's president asked to see solid performance data on the 200 managers likely to be affected by the changes. It did not exist. For one-third of managers performance data was more than two years old. For others it was more current but was incomplete.

The human resources staff, under pressure of time to restructure, and commited to use the new quality improvement methodology, created over the next four months a manual 360-degree feedback data gathering system. Data from this was used to make restructuring decisions. Everyone involved vowed never to be in this situation again. This created the catalyst for building a state-of-the-art performance management system with the strong support of the senior management team. A further stimulus was the realisation that PRC was moving towards a team-based structure with fewer managers and larger spans of control, up from 1:5 to 1:10. This meant that it would become more difficult to rely solely on top-down performance assessment, requiring more of a multi-rater approach.

After designing and piloting the questionnaire and selecting a processing system, the implementation team began the new programme with careful communication and education, initially to the top 50 executives, followed by 500 managers six months later. Because this was such a huge departure from the hierarchical approach of previous years, PRC wisely decided that easing into this methodology would be the most prudent approach. It began by having the 360-degree feedback data used strictly for development purposes and connecting it to pay after one annual review cycle.

Using a continuous improvement approach, each pilot yielded new lessons – which were duly incorporated. Focus groups were used to develop and refine the questionnaire, and also to brief managers about the programme. Both approaches were generally held to have lessened the resistance to change.

After the executive pilot and the management pilot, PRC decided to implement one of the most exciting features of the process. Because they have systems integration and consultancy experience in interactive voice response (IVR) technology, PRC decided to use an IVR product to enter the 360-degree feedback data directly into the processing system. This was crucial in creating a system that was easy and cost effective to administer, convenient for employees, and which met data security and quality requirements.

Respondent team selection packages are sent to each participant with instructions to choose up to 13 team members (including the self). Employees must ask the prospective team members' permission before putting them on their team. The data is then entered into the team selection system and questionnaires are generated for each evaluation.

Each respondent receives a questionnaire. The single piece of paper contains the questions (33) and the rating scale (six points). It also gives the names of the participants for this respondent to evaluate. The questionnaire is in the form of a worksheet which asks respondents to score each participant against each question. They then use any touch-tone telephone, tap in their PIN number, and follow simple spoken instructions from the system to input their scores on each participant via the telephone. Each respondent then reviews the scores before locking them and exiting the system. There is a direct helpline within the company for those who have queries or problems. If the respondent is interrupted or disconnected they can call back and be returned immediately to the point where they left off.

The advantages of such a system are clear: other than the central processing system, no special equipment (eg a personal computer) is required. Geographical dispersal of participants and respondents is not a problem because they can use any telephone anywhere in the country. The actual equipment used is very familiar to everyone.

To preserve confidentiality the employee destroys the questionnaire. The accuracy of transposition is maximised by encouraging respondents to verify their responses before system closure.

The performance measurement system as it stands now provides a balanced performance appraisal. It consists of three parts as Table 26 shows.

Table 26

THREE STAGES OF APPRAISAL

PRC's total performance management process is composed of:	
Part One	Behaviour assessment using the 360-degree feedback tool includes three phases: team selection, evaluation and feedback
Part Two	Key assignments and objectives
Part Three	Individual development plan
The results of Part One will be combined with the results of Part Two to obtain your overall performance category.	

The first part consists of the measurement of behaviours, 'soft' measures, and competencies, ie process or 'How' measured on a 360-degree feedback basis by several raters. The second part – results or 'What' – comprises a more conventional appraisal by the boss, based on harder measures, results, achievements and so on.

There are three phases to the behavioural portion (Part One) of the system. Detailed procedures are shown below.

Phase one – Team selection

☐ Introduction by senior vice-president – human resources.

☐ Participants receive respondent team selection package that includes important dates in the total performance management process.

☐ Pre-assessment training packages are available.

☐ The participant selects a feedback team of 13 people (including self). The participant's boss has to approve the balance and make-up of the team. A well-balanced assessment team consists of the boss, an indirect boss, direct reports, peers/colleagues, and self. (While the self-assessment shows up in the report, it does not count in the tabulation of performance rating. Out of the 12 respondents the high and low scores are omitted from the calculations. If there are less than three respondents in a category, the software will not report, to protect anonymity.)

☐ The feedback team is entered into the database.

Phase two – Evaluation

☐ Human Resources distributes paper questionnaires to participants and respondents.

☐ Respondents complete and phone-in their confidential results (total time three minutes after survey completion). They may also use an intranet to enter their ratings.

☐ Participants phone-in their self-rating (this is recorded but does not count towards pay calculations).

☐ Stragglers are chased up by voice-mail and e-mail.

☐ Survey results are processed in-house and feedback reports are produced.

Phase three – Feedback

☐ Feedback reports are sent to bosses.

☐ Bosses give the report to employees one week prior to a performance discussion.

☐ Employee completes a questionnaire analysing the results and identifies strengths and areas needing development.

☐ The employee then attends a post-assessment training session to assist them with the interpretation of results and give guidance in preparing an individual development plan.

After the employee receives the results from Part One (the 'How' part of the review) and Part Two (the 'What' part of the balanced review) the company provides additional resources that the individual can draw upon. For example, managers receive training in giving feedback and coaching. Employees are encouraged to gather additional feedback from the team on how to make better use of strengths and improvement suggestions.

Link to pay

The results of Part One, behaviour assessment, are combined with the results of Part Two, key assignments and objectives, to obtain the overall performance category that is linked to decisions on salary and bonus.

A chart shows how both 'How' and 'What' are combined to produce the overall performance category. The principle is that the highest rating can be earned only through equally strong performance on both process and results. A low score in either area will significantly reduce the performance rating.

Impact on the organisation

Under the new system, PRC enjoys 100 per cent participation on Part One, behaviour assessment. The USA is a country very prone to employee litigation, yet in three years there have been no legal charges stemming from performance review challenges. Employee confidence with, and buy-in to, the system is high. This has allowed the human resources function to shift its emphasis from one-to-one arbitration and reactive employee relations to more proactive, highly valued work. The quality of the data generated is much improved, contributing to a more factual and informed management approach.

14

LONDON BOROUGH OF CROYDON

Using 360-degree feedback in evaluating a training and organisation development project

The London Borough of Croydon is the largest of 33 London boroughs, providing services – including education, social services, housing, libraries and leisure, public services and works – for over 326,800 residents and 140,000 households. It covers an area of 32 square miles, of which roughly a third is open space and green belt. Croydon is located approximately 12 miles from the centre of London. In addition, a large number of shoppers and workers regularly travel to Croydon.

In 1993 a facilities management business unit was created (Office Facilities) bringing together a wide range of support services to the central civic offices and outstations. This included office services, eg telephones, mailroom, reprographics, one-stop and text processing. It also included services to the building including maintenance, catering, cleaning and porterage. Service-level agreements were formulated to determine the level of service provision and charging structure together with performance targets. The staffing level at that time was approximately 135. In addition, an in-house employment agency was introduced to provide temporary staff to all departments.

Since that time there has been even greater pressure to improve services and at the same time make efficiency savings.

The office facilities department engaged an external consultant to carry out a total quality development programme using the 'VALUE' model described ovearleaf. The department had previously obtained BS5750 registration and had done extensive work on developing quality systems. As a follow-up activity, the manager of the department identified a need to concentrate more on quality attitudes and practices. The VALUE model was used to tailor a programme for the department.

The VALUE model consists of five elements, considered to be the key constituents of an effective total quality culture.

The VALUE programme was run on the basis of a one-day workshop each month during much of 1995. The whole of the management team of office facilities, 24 managers and supervisors, took part. The workshops were a mixture of theory around the VALUE model and practical workshops, supported by projects and other work that went on between sessions.

For the purposes of practical work, both during and between workshops, team members worked in sub-groups of between four and seven people. In this way each team member was able to maximise their contribution – something that does not always happen in a larger team. It also allows team members

Table 27

FIVE ELEMENTS OF VALUE

Vision involves the creation of a coherent strategic perspective for the organisation or organisational unit concerned. It deals with how to create involvement in putting together a vision. It also examines how to make the vision a force for change within the organisation.

Assurance concerns the attitudes and practices of the organisation in relation to its customers, both external and internal. It examines the ways in which the needs of customers are researched and customer specifications put together. It defines what steps the organisation needs to take to assure the customer that the outputs delivered actually meet the specifications as defined. This also includes quality practices within the organisation.

Leadership concerns the specific practices of leadership that are necessary to bring about a quality-focused culture, quality improvement, and the involvement of all employees.

Unity addresses the use of teamworking. It applies both to normal operational teams and specialist teams, such as problem-solving or quality improvement groups. It creates a unified and cohesive approach to quality working within the organisation.

Evaluation looks at the ways in which the organisation assesses its performance in the context of performance indicators within the unit concerned. It involves the use of other forms of comparison, such as benchmarking with other external organisations or departments. It is concerned with how data on results is used to improve quality assurance and update the vision, thus completing the cycle.

© Ward Dutton Partnership

to understand and value better the contribution they could make, providing encouragement to contribute in the future.

The leadership part of the VALUE programme uses two 360-degree feedback instruments – the management interpersonal skills survey (MISS) and the individual development survey (IDS). The MISS is designed to examine nine competencies that cover the general area of managing people, such as motivating, empowerment and delegating. The IDS has eleven non-management competencies, such as initiative-taking, technical competency and communicating. It aims to help participants maximise their relationships and enhance their professional development.

The questionnaire consists of three basic questions:

☐ Importance: how important is this area of your job?
☐ Current performance: how much of this behaviour do you see now?
☐ Expected performance: how much of this behaviour do you expect to see?

In the feedback report the first section, on importance ratings, reveals how critical each of the competencies covered by the MISS or IDS is to that particular person in their current role. This allows the participant to understand which areas require discussion or clarification with others. It is especially useful in revealing discrepancies between the views of the participant and those of their boss. The software used generates the word

Figure 24

IMPORTANCE CHART

Skill area	N	AVG	Average rating 1 2 3 4 5 6 7 8 9	Priority	Recommendation
1. Delegating					
Self	1	5.0			
Boss A	1	7.0		2nd	
Staff/Support A	3	9.0		1st	CLARIFY
Peers A	2	5.0			

© CCI Assessment and Development Group

CLARIFY automatically whenever there is a large gap between self-ratings and those given by another person or group.

The next section is a detailed analysis, question by question, of the gaps between respondents' rating on the 'current' scale compared to their rating on the 'expected' scale.

The scores shown in the report are the average gap sizes (AGS) between these two scales. A large number indicates that too little (or too much) behaviour is seen by raters. A small number indicates that the participant is meeting expectations and is therefore effective in this particular behaviour. Useful comments are again generated automatically in the Recommendations column: four stars for a strong performer, two for a small gap and the word INCREASE where improvement is clearly required.

All 24 participants took part in the feedback programme. They received feedback based on the results of either the MISS or IDS data. The programme managers used this along with discussions about the importance of leadership, issues to do with leadership style and behaviour, and how leadership could influence the development of quality within the department. Participants left the workshops with a personal development plan and with some specific commitments that would help the team forward. At that time the team committed itself to a reassessment after a period long enough to allow them to work on their development needs.

The reassessment was carried out some six months after the end of the programme, using the same questionnaires, and where possible, the same respondents. The purpose was to give

Figure 25

CURRENT v EXPECTED PERFORMANCE

Analysis by behaviour

Behaviour	N	AGS	Average gap size C–E 1 2 3 4 5	Gaps 0 1 2 3 4	Recommendation
43. Support the decisions you make					
Self	1	0.00	I	I	* * * *
Boss A	1	1.00	C ■■■ ►E	I	* *
Staff/Support A	3	2.00	C ■■■■■ ►E	I I I	INCREASE
Peers A	2	1.00	C ■■■ ►E	2	* *

© CCI Assessment and Development Group

further feedback to participants, and to evaluate how far the department had progressed.

On receipt of their second set of feedback results, participants were delighted to find that the areas they had specifically identified in their action plans were indeed improving in the eyes of their respondents.

In addition to general improvements on all fronts, a further analysis revealed that 10 participants who had completed the MISS had managed to reduce their average gap size by more than a third – statistically a highly significant improvement in the team management interpersonal skills.

Another important finding was in the differences in how each respondent group rated participants. This reflects the ability of 360-degree feedback to give the complete picture on performance. Staff rated participants much more harshly than did bosses, while peers and self were somewhere in-between. The differences can be seen on the graph in Figure 26.

Interestingly, it was the self and peers who observed the largest change in participants' skills between the two occasions. It was concluded that follow-up activity should focus on partici-

Figure 26

AVERAGE RATINGS BY GROUPS

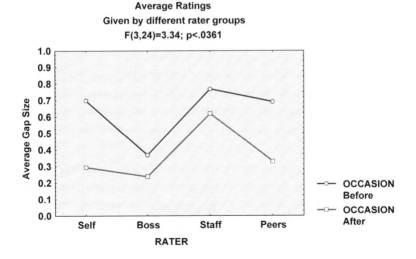

Average Ratings
Given by different rater groups
$F_{(3,24)} = 3.34$; $p < .0361$

pants' behaviour with their staff, as this was the area requiring most improvement.

Clearly, one would hope that over time the gap sizes would reduce, indicating an improvement in behaviour as a result of the development programme, and observed by the respondents.

Without this data, the organisation and those running the programme would have little idea of how effective it would have been. They would not have known about individual improvement on specific behaviours, nor would they have realised that the participants were seen differently by different groups. They would therefore have had no indicators of its value and no pointers to what further development work was required.

However, armed with this information, they were able to take informed decisions about future developments, including extending the programme to other departments, confident that it would produce results.

Appendices

Appendix A

INSTRUCTIONS FOR

PARTICIPANTS

THE DEVELOPING PRINCIPALS

FEEDBACK PROCESS

1. Identify the people from whom you will be receiving feedback

Selecting the people that you believe can make accurate judgements about the skills examined in the Developing Principals questionnaire is an important part of the process. Some guidelines that will help you to choose appropriate respondents are:

☐ You should complete a questionnaire on yourself.

☐ A Partner should complete a questionnaire. You may also identify a second Partner or a Mentor.

☐ A selection of clients should be asked to complete questionnaires. This group should be chosen from your most recent clients and should include your largest client in the last 12 months (in terms of time spent working for them). Identify the person (or people) within each client organisation that you have had the most contact with, as they will be most able to comment on your skills. You must identify at least three clients, in order to maintain their anonymity.

☐ Others chosen to complete questionnaires on your performance should be colleagues or support staff that you have worked with closely in recent months. The important factor is that they have worked with you closely enough to have observed your recent performance. You must identify at least three others in order to maintain their anonymity.

2. Fill in the front of your own form

On the front of your own form there is space for you to fill in the name of each respondent you have chosen. Make sure that you enter their names in the appropriate groups, or your feedback report may be confusing.

3. Fill in the front of the other forms

On each other form, fill in your own name and the name of the respondent that you are sending it to. Place the form in an envelope with a respondent letter (you may wish to add your own message to the standard wording) and a bureau service envelope.

You are now ready to mail your forms

While only one feedback report will be produced and given to you, Partners will inevitably be interested in the results and in the action plan that you create as a result of this process. It is recommended that you share your feedback with a Partner as this will help your relationship and your development. The processing agency follows strict guidelines regarding best practice and will not divulge details of an individual's report to Coopers and Lybrand.

Appendix B

Coopers
&Lybrand

**Developing
Principals**

Participant

Name _____

Respondent

Name _____

This questionnaire is part of a development exercise. The information you give will be used only by the individual who sent it to you, and will not be held by the firm in any form. To help this person make the most of the feedback please use as much of the five-point scale as you can. Your responses will be kept strictly confidential. You will not be identified to the person who sent you this survey.

- ☐ Please make sure that your own name and the name of the participant (the person you are rating) are written clearly on this page.

- ☐ This is not a test, there are no right or wrong answers. Please attempt to use the entire scale.

- ☐ Completely fill the circle with a heavy black mark and erase all stray marks, eg ① ● ③ ④ ⑤ ○

Please return the completed questionnaire to the following address by:

_____

If you have any queries do not hesitate to contact

_____

Appendix C

Coopers &Lybrand | **Developing Principals**

Participant

Name _____ 0

Partner

Name _____ 1   Name _____ 2

Others

Name _____ 30   Name _____ 33

Name _____ 31   Name _____ 34

Name _____ 32   Name _____ 35

Clients

Name _____ 40   Name _____ 43

Name _____ 41   Name _____ 44

Name _____ 42   Name _____ 45

This questionnaire is part of a development exercise. The information you give will be used only by the individual who sent it to you, and will not be held by the firm in any form. To help this person make the most of the feedback please use as much of the five-point scale as you can. Your responses will be kept strictly confidential. You will not be identified to the person who sent you this survey.

- □ Please make sure that your own name and the name of the participant (the person you are rating) are written clearly on this page.
- □ This is not a test, there are no right or wrong answers. Please attempt to use the entire scale.
- □ Completely fill the circle with a heavy black mark and erase all stray marks, eg ① ● ③ ④ ⑤   ○

Please return the completed questionnaire to the following address by:

_____

If you have any queries do not hesitate to contact

_____

Appendix D

Dear Colleague,

360-degree feedback: Developing Principals

Coopers and Lybrand is committed to the development of all of its staff, and encourages each individual to improve continuously. I have been offered the opportunity to use a technique known as 360-degree feedback to help me prioritise my ongoing development. Using this questionnaire-based method, I hope to receive some really frank and useful feedback on my job performance from the people that I work with.

During our work together, you will have been in a unique position to observe my work behaviour, which is why I would value your input. Please take the time to complete the enclosed questionnaire, returning it by _____ in the envelope provided, to the processing agency (an external data-processing organisation).

Your response will be grouped together with others, so that it is impossible for me to identify what you said from what others have said. This is done to protect your anonymity, and to allow you to be completely frank in your response.

Thank you very much for providing me with this feedback, which I will try to respond to by improving my performance in the areas highlighted as highest priority. Your co-operation is appreciated.

Yours sincerely,

Please note that the due date is _____

Appendix E

Evaluation of 360-degree feedback

This two part questionnaire evaluates the 360-degree feedback project. 360-degree feedback is a significant investment of management time and effort for our organisation. Please provide further feedback for us to determine whether we are maximising the return on this particular investment.

The questionnaire has two parts. Part One asks questions about your views and experiences as a manager who has received feedback from subordinates, and your views about future usage of the 360-degree feedback tool. Part Two asks questions about your views and experiences as a direct report of a manager who has been through the 360-degree feedback process.

The questionnaire may be completed anonymously, although if you wish, you can put your name to the questionnaire. No remarks will be attributable to individuals in any reports that are produced.

Evaluation of 360-degree feedback

Part one
To be completed by managers who have received 360-degree feedback

Name (do not complete if you wish to remain anonymous)

Q1. When, approximately, did you receive your 360-degree feedback report?

M	M	Y	Y

Q2. Which one of the following statements most accurately reflects your currently held views about 360-degree feedback?

☐ There is no link between the achievement of my business goals and the way that I perform as a manager ☐

☐ There is a link between the achievement of my business goals and the way that I perform as a manager *and* 360-degree feedback will help me to achieve my goals ☐

☐ There is a link between the achievement of my business goals and the way that I perform as a manager *but* 360-degree feedback will not help me to achieve my goals ☐

Q3. As a result of your 360-degree feedback, were you surprised by any hidden strengths or weaknesses revealed to you by your direct or second level subordinates?

Yes, they revealed hidden strengths ☐

Yes, they revealed hidden weaknesses ☐

Yes, they revealed both hidden strengths and weaknesses ☐

No, there were no surprises in my report ☐

Q4. Did you have a discussion with your manager to share any part of your 360-degree feedback and action plan?

Yes ☐

No ☐

Q5. Have you shared your feedback report with your team members who provided input to the exercise?

Yes ☐

No ☐

Q6. Did your manager share their feedback report with you?

Yes ☐

No ☐

Q7. Did your manager share their action plan with you?

Yes ☐

No ☐

Q8a. Is the feedback report easy to understand and interpret?

Yes   ☐ ⟶ Now go to Q9

No   ☐ ⟶ Answer Q8b

Q8b. In what ways could the report be improved? *(write in below)*

```



```

Q9a. Do you believe that the guarantee of confidentiality given to you, as a participant in 360-degree feedback has been observed throughout the process?

Yes   ☐ ⟶ Now go to Q10

No   ☐ ⟶ Answer Q9b

Q9b. Why do you think the guarantee of confidentiality has not been observed?

```



```

Q10. Do you believe that the right approach is to guarantee anonymity *in all respects* to respondents who complete the 360-degree feedback questionnaires?

Yes   ☐ ⟶ Now go to Q12

No   ☐ ⟶ Answer Q11a

Q11a. In your opinion would 360-degree feedback be improved by attributing verbatim comments to the person who made them?

Yes   ☐

No   ☐

Q11b. Why do you think 360-degree feedback would/would not be improved? (*write in below*)

```


```

Q12. In your opinion should the facilitator to the feedback interview be from the same business as yourself, or from a different business?

From the same business I work in ☐

From a different business ☐

Makes no difference ☐

Q13a. Do you think it should be mandatory for all managers, with four or more employees working for them, to go through the process of 360-degree feedback?

Yes ☐

No ☐

Q13b. Why do you think it should/should not be mandatory? (*write in below*)

```


```

Q14a. Should it be mandatory for all supervisors with four or more employees to go through the process of 360-degree feedback?

Yes ☐

No ☐

Q14b. Why do you think it should/should not be mandatory? (*write in below*)

```


```

Q15. How would you rate the overall quality of the facilitator of the feedback process that you personally experienced?

Excellent ☐

Very Good ☐

Good ☐

Poor ☐

Very Poor ☐

Terrible ☐

Q16. Following your participation in 360-degree feedback, what impact has there been on your commitment to personal change?

My commitment has increased ☐

My commitment has not changed ☐

My commitment has decreased ☐

Q17a. Do you support the possibility of linking *future* 360-degree feedback results to elements of managers' remuneration (bonus and/or basic salary)?

I strongly support the possibility ☐

I support the possibility ☐

I do not support the possibility ☐

I do not support the possibility at all ☐

Q17b. Why do you support/not support the possibility?

Q18a. As a result of your 360-degree feedback have you changed the way that you work at all?

Yes ☐ ⟶ Answer Q18b

No ☐ ⟶ Now go to Q19

Q18b. What are you now doing differently?

```



```

Q19. If you have any further comments to make about the feedback questionnaires please write them below.

```




```

Q20. Have you completed a questionnaire about your manager?

Yes ☐ ➤ *Please complete part two of this questionnaire*

No   ☐ ➤ *Thank you for completing this questionnaire*

Evaluation of 360-degree feedback

Part two
To be completed only if you have completed a questionnaire about your manager.

Q1. When, approximately, did you complete the questionnaire about your manager?

M	M	Y	Y

Q2. Did your manager share their feedback report with you?

Yes ☐

No   ☐

Q3. Did your manager share their action plan with you?

Yes   ☐

No   ☐

Q4a. Have you noticed your manager doing anything differently which you would attribute to their participation in 360-degree feedback feedback?

Yes   ☐ ———————► Answer Q4b

No   ☐ ———————► Now go to Q6

Q4b. What things have you noticed your manager doing differently?

```
┌─────────────────────────────────────────────────┐
│                                                   │
│                                                   │
│                                                   │
│                                                   │
│                                                   │
└─────────────────────────────────────────────────┘
```

Q5. Have these changes that you noticed been sustained to date?

Yes   ☐

No   ☐

Q6a. In your opinion should your manager continue to receive 360-degree feedback at regular intervals in the future?

Yes   ☐ ———————► How often should this happen?

```
┌─────────────────────────────────────────┐
│                                           │
└─────────────────────────────────────────┘
```

No   ☐

Q6b. Why do you think your manager should/should not receive 360-degree feedback at regular intervals? (write in below)

```
┌─────────────────────────────────────────────────┐
│                                                   │
│                                                   │
│                                                   │
│                                                   │
└─────────────────────────────────────────────────┘
```

Q7. A guarantee was given to subordinates who completed questionnaires that their responses would be anonymous. Do you feel that your anonymity as a contributor was preserved?

Yes ☐

No ☐

Don't know ☐

Q8. On future occasions when your manager participates in 360-degree feedback would you be willing to have any verbatim comments you make clearly identified as your comments?

Yes ☐

No ☐

If you have any further comments to make about the questionnaires please write them below.

☐

Evaluation of 360-degree feedback – facilitator review

The following questions should be used to structure the interviews with facilitators participating in the 360-degree feedback programme.

Name of facilitator: _____

Q1. Do you believe the 360-degree feedback programme is linked to the achievement of our business and organisational objectives?

Q2. Do you feel that the training provided for your participation as a facilitator was adequate?

Q3. On average how long did your preparation take for a facilitation feedback session?

Q4. How long did the feedback sessions take on average?

Q5. Were you unprepared for everything that happened during the feedback sessions?

Q6. Did you draw up an action plan before the end of the facilitation session?

Q7. Have you maintained contact with the people to whom you have provided feedback?

Q8. Did you feel comfortable in the role of facilitator?

Q9. What benefits did your participants express about the exercise?

Q10. What criticisms did your participants express about the exercise?

Q11. How commited to the process do you feel the participants were?

Q12. If the organisation was to repeat the exercise, what frequency do you believe would be appropriate for the programme?

Q13. What improvements/changes would you recommend be made to the process?

Q14. Do you believe the facilitators should be totally independent of the person being fed back to, or drawn from within their own business?

Q15. How would you rate the overall value of the 360-degree feed-back programme?

Q16. Are there any other comments or views you would wish to make?

INDEX